The Struggle
Against
Terrorism

EDITED BY

William P. Lineberry

NOTICE TO REFERENCE SHELF SUBSCRIBERS

An error occurs in Reference Shelf Volume 49, Number 1, *Canada in Transition*, which was published in April of 1977. Lines 10 and 11 of page 72 describe Edgar Z. Friedenberg as ". . . an American who gave up his citizenship in order to become a citizen of Canada." The corrected sentence should read ". . . an American who is a permanent resident of Canada."

Please cut out the corrected paragraph below and substitute it for the first paragraph on page 72:

Canada is a nation of great diversity, and this diversity manifests itself in the Canadian political environment. In many ways the Canadian political scene can be likened to that of the United States—often characterized by divisions and infighting based upon social, economic, and sectional differences. Canadians, however, differ from Americans in regard to their respective expectations concerning what, if any, benefits should be derived from their political systems. This idea is dealt with in the first article, written by Edgar Z. Friedenberg, an American who is a permanent resident of Canada.

Canada is a nation of great diversity, and this diversity manifests itself in the Canadian political environment. In particular, the Canadian political scene cannot be understood in terms of the United States election campaigns and by domestic infighting based upon social, economic and structural (Cultural) conditions, however, differ from American in regard to their respective expectations concerning what, if any, benefits should be derived from their political systems. This chapter is dealt with in the following guide, within by being less fundamental an American with a permanent resident of Canada.

THE STRUGGLE

AGAINST

TERRORISM

edited by WILLIAM P. LINEBERRY

THE REFERENCE SHELF
Volume 49   Number 3

THE H. W. WILSON COMPANY
New York   1977

THE REFERENCE SHELF

The books in this series contain reprints of articles, excerpts from books, and addresses on current issues and social trends in the United States and other countries. There are six separately bound numbers in each volume, all of which are generally published in the same calendar year. One number is a collection of recent speeches; each of the others is devoted to a single subject and gives background information and discussion from various points of view, concluding with a comprehensive bibliography. Books in the series may be purchased individually or on subscription.

Copyright © 1977
By The H. W. Wilson Company
PRINTED IN THE UNITED STATES OF AMERICA

Library of Congress Cataloging in Publication Data
Main entry under title:

The Struggle against terrorism.

(The Reference shelf ; v. 49, no. 3)

Bibliography: p.

1. Terrorism—Addresses, essays, lectures.
I. Lineberry, William P. II. Series.

JX5420.S77   301.6′33   77-22819
ISBN 0-8242-0605-3

PREFACE

Thirty-two years since the end of World War II the menace of global conflict continues to plague us. And now a new specter has risen to haunt our times: the specter of random violence—of sudden, brutal death at the hands of psychotics or political fanatics whose cause or grievance is remote or unknown to the victims of their wrath. As the *Economist* of London observed with appropriate irony some years ago:

> If you are filled with rage because the twentieth century is as imperfect as the others, or because the injustice that hurts you most has not been removed from the world, or just because you cannot get other people to agree with you, you are entitled to grab the first person you see on the street and hold him at gunpoint in a cellar until the government buys you off.

Such, indeed, is the basic nature of modern terrorism, a phenomenon variously described in the pages of this compilation as a "theater of fear," a "weapon of the weak," and "propaganda of the deed." It is a phenomenon that feeds, ironically, on the best that modern civilization has to offer by way of mass communications and advanced technology. Were it not for the gleaming jet airplanes that seem to be favorite targets and the TV cameras that rivet world attention on such exploits, many a terrorist might well be at home. The worry, pointed up in these pages, is that this disease of our time may someday soon involve nuclear blackmail and the loss of not just one or two hundred lives but a million or more.

We live in what Yonah Alexander, professor of international studies at the State University of New York, has called "the age of terror," and the purpose of this volume is to examine the nature of modern terrorism, to place it in historical perspective, to debate its meaning and portent for

our lives, and to examine what is being done and what
more is being proposed to bring terrorism to a halt. Although there is little evidence here to suggest that terrorist
tactics have proved successful in the achievement of their
aims, almost every author in this volume expresses the fear
that the use of such tactics will continue to spread. The
more technologically sophisticated modern society becomes,
the more vulnerable it appears to grow to terrorist whims.
Perhaps this is what Rousseau meant in saying that every
civilization carries within itself the causes of its own destruction.

How serious is the problem of terrorism, and how far
should governments be prepared to go in dealing with it?
What causes terrorism, and what is feeding its growth? Is
terrorism ever morally justified? What does it tell us about
the moral state of society, generally?

These are some of the questions that this compilation
seeks to address. Section I broadly examines the nature of
terrorism, tracing its roots back through what David Fromkin, author and lawyer, calls the time of the assassins to the
French Revolution. Section II treats the modern phenomenon in greater detail, examining the varieties of terrorism
currently afflicting the world. Section III presents contend-
ing views on the moral justification for terrorism and on its
effectiveness. Section IV discusses efforts currently under
way to combat terrorism, and the concluding section analyzes further means by which we can come to grips with the
problem. Although the issue of so-called "state terrorism"—
i.e., terrorism practiced by repressive governments against
their own nationals or other states—occasionally enters into
the discussion in these pages, that issue opens the subject far
beyond the confines of this volume.

The compiler wishes to thank the many authors and publishers who have courteously granted permission for the reprinting of their materials in this book.

WILLIAM P. LINEBERRY

June 1977

NOTE TO THE READER

Several articles in this compilation touch on the death penalty as a deterrent to terrorism. More detailed discussion of this is to be found in Irwin Isenberg's *The Death Penalty* (Reference Shelf, Volume 49, Number 2) published in June 1977.

CONTENTS

I. LIVING WITH RANDOM VIOLENCE

EDITOR'S INTRODUCTION

What are the crucial elements in modern terrorism? There is, first of all, the grievance—real or imagined—and the fanaticism basic to the use of terrorist means toward seeking redress. Then there are the many vulnerable targets available in open societies where liberties of expression and movement can tip the scales against the requirements of public order and security. There is also the fascination on the part of the mass media with the obvious human drama involved. Finally, and most crucially, there is the response to the terrorist's deed, even if it comes as a flat rejection of whatever demand is made. The articles in this section survey the nature and history of terrorism as we know it today.

As the opening article, written by lawyer-author David Fromkin for *Foreign Affairs,* points out, it is the terrorist's ability to provoke a dramatic response from both public opinion and concerned authorities that gives him the upper hand in a scenario of his own devising. The whole point of terrorism, in short, is that it must not be ignored, and in that sense the overreaction of press, public, and governments to terrorist exploits helps perpetuate a phenomenon that claims far fewer lives than those taken by reckless drivers in any given year. The only inherently valuable aspect of an outrageous act is its worth in capturing attention, and mass attention getting appears to be nine tenths of the terrorist's game. Terrorism is calculated to generate fear which, in turn, conditions the response to terrorist demands. By responding in ways other than expected, authorities can, Fromkin suggests, beat the terrorist at his own game.

In the second article, two editors of *Reader's Digest* describe the mushrooming of terrorist exploits and warn that more trouble lies ahead. In the third, a reporter for *The Christian Science Monitor* details the apparent powerlessness of governments and international organizations in the face of the problem.

The section concludes with a *U.S. News & World Report* interview with Robert A. Fearey (formerly of the United States Department of State), the man charged in 1975 with coordination of antiterrorist activities for the United States, explaining why Washington has adopted a "no-concessions" policy with respect to terrorist demands. The interview tells why prevention and punishment are the best deterrents.

TERRORISM: ORIGINS AND STRATEGY [1]

The grim events at the Athens airport on August 5, 1973, were in a sense symbolic. Dreadfully real to those who were involved, the occurrences of that day also transcended their own reality, somewhat as myths do, epitomizing an entire aspect of contemporary existence in one specific drama.

When the hand grenades were hurled into the departure lounge and the machine gunners simultaneously mowed down the passengers waiting to embark for New York City, it seemed incomprehensible that so harmless a group should be attacked. The merest glance at their hand-luggage, filled with snorkels and cameras, would have shown that they had spent their time in such peaceful pursuits as swimming, sunbathing, and snapping photos of the Parthenon.

The raid had been undertaken on behalf of an Arab Palestine. Yet the airport passengers had done the Arabs no harm. Their journey had only been to Greece. Palestine had nothing to do with them; it was another country, across the sea, and its problems were not of their making. More-

[1] From "The Strategy of Terrorism," by David Fromkin, attorney-at-law, author of *The Question of Government*. *Foreign Affairs*. 53:683-98. Jl. '75. Reprinted by permission from *Foreign Affairs*, July 1975. Copyright 1975 by Council on Foreign Relations, Inc.

over, Athens was a capital friendly to the Arab cause—as was Paris, the scene of more recent airline attacks.

Similar incidents have occurred with terrible frequency throughout the 1960s and 1970s. The generations that have come to maturity in Europe and America since the end of the Second World War have asked only to bask in the sunshine of a summertime world; but increasingly they have been forced instead to live in the fearful shadow of other people's deadly quarrels. Gangs of politically motivated gunmen have disrupted everyday life, intruding and forcing their parochial feuds upon the unwilling attention of everybody else.

True, other ages have suffered from crime and outrage, but what we are experiencing today goes beyond such things. Too small to impose their will by military force, terrorist bands nonetheless are capable nowadays of causing enough damage to intimidate and blackmail the governments of the world. Only modern technology makes this possible—the bazooka, the plastic bomb, the submachine gun, and perhaps, over the horizon, the nuclear mini-bomb. The transformation has enabled terrorism to enter the political arena on a new scale, and to express ideological goals of an organized sort rather than mere crime, madness, or emotional derangement as in the past.

Political terrorism is a distinctive disorder of the modern world. It originated as a term and, arguably, as a practice, less than two centuries ago and has come into the spotlight of global conflict in our lifetime. Whereas both organized and irregular (or guerrilla) warfare began with the human race, political terrorism emerged as a concept only in 1793. As a political strategy, it is both new and original; and if I am correct, its nature has not yet fully been appreciated.

Of course nobody can remain unaware of the upsurge of global terrorism that has occurred in recent years. But the novelty of it has not been perceived. Force usually generates fear, and fear is usually an additional weapon. But terrorism employs the weapon of fear in a special and complicated sort of way.

Rule by Fear

The disassociation of fear from force in the context of organized politics emerged first in the Reign of Terror, the episode (1793–1794) during the history of revolutionary France from which the English and French words for terrorism derive. The terrorists in question were, of course, Robespierre and his satellites, St. Just and Couthon. Sitting as a faction in the Committee of Public Safety, their accusations of treason sent victims to the guillotine in droves. By the mere threat of accusation against their fellow committee members, they used the entire committee, thus united, in order to dominate the National Convention and the other public bodies of the French Republic.

Robespierre was overthrown when his system was used against him. His mistake was in letting Joseph Fouché know that he was the next intended victim; and Fouché, the wily intriguer who later became Napoleon's minister of police, made the best possible use of his few remaining days. He persuaded the feuding, rival politicians of his day that they had to unite against the triumvirs or else face execution one by one; fear of the regime should cause them not to serve it, but to overthrow it. On 8 Thermidor (July 26, 1794) Robespierre made another mistake when he told the Convention that he had prepared a new list of traitors in their midst—and then refused to tell them whose names were on the list. Fouché's warnings were confirmed, and his counsel was heeded. When Robespierre entered the National Convention late in the stormy summer morning of 9 Thermidor, he found a mob of delegates united by the determination to murder him before he could murder them; and that was the end of him.

Robespierre had coerced a nation of 27 million people into accepting his dictatorship. His followers sent many thousands either to jail or to their deaths; one scholar's esti-

mate is 40,000 deaths and 300,000 arrests. Yet when retribution came and Robespierre and his group of supporters
were executed, it turned out that in all there were only 22
of them.

Of course it is not meant to suggest that this is the whole
story of the French Terror. Yet what emerges most strongly
from any account of these events is the dramatic disparity
between the objective weakness of the Robespierre faction,
whose numbers were few and whose military resources were
limited, and their immense subjective power, which allowed
them to kill, imprison, or control so many. There was no
need to fear the triumvirs other than the fact that other people feared them and therefore would execute their orders.
Their power was unreal; it was an illusionist's trick. No
citadels had to be stormed, no armies had to be crushed, in
order to overthrow them. If the public ignored what they
said, then the terrorists went back to being political no-
bodies. Their dictatorship vanished in an instant when
Robespierre and his colleagues were prevented from reaching the speakers' platform on 9 Thermidor.

In the end, the terrorists overreached themselves, and
men saw through them and stood up to them. Then—and
only then—it became clear that France had never had anything to fear from them other than fear itself.

Turning Terror Against Government

Perhaps the closest parallel to Robespierre's method was
that followed by the late Senator Joseph McCarthy in 1950–
1954. Like Robespierre, McCarthy claimed to have lists of
traitors whose names he would not immediately reveal, and
many did his will in order to avoid being accused by him of
treason or of lack of patriotism. And, like Robespierre's, his
power stopped when he went too far and Joseph Welch, his
Fouché, stood up to him on television. But McCarthy never
seized supreme power in the country, nor did his accusations send people to the guillotine. In that sense it can be
said that Robespierre has had no successors.

Since his time, in fact, political terrorism has become especially notorious in a different cause from that in which Robespierre used it. It has been used to destroy governments rather than to sustain them. This changed the way in which many people thought of it as a political strategy and how they viewed its adherents. As revolutionaries, terrorists have come to seem romantic figures to many. Their life of dangers and disguises, risks and betrayals, conspiracies and secret societies, exerted a powerful fascination. As torn and tormented characters, they provided authors with the stuff of which complex and interesting novels can be made.

Though the terrorists seemed romantic, until recently they also seemed ineffective. Until the Irish Treaty of 1921, they scored no significant political successes. The most famous of the terrorist groups up to that time was the Terrorist Brigade of the Russian Socialists-Revolutionists; and not merely did they fail to change the Tsarist government in the ways in which they desired, they also failed to pick up the pieces when it was overthrown by others. Plekhanov, Lenin, Trotsky and the other Russian disciples of Marx had seen more clearly in placing their emphasis on mass organization rather than on individual terrorism. The Bolsheviks came to power by winning the metropolitan workmen, the sailors of the Baltic fleet, and the soldiers to their side. Organization proved to be the key to victory. It was not individual gunmen but armed masses who seized power in Russia. Revolution, like war, is the strategy of the strong; terrorism is the strategy of the weak.

It is an uncertain and indirect strategy that employs the weapon of fear in a special sort of way in which to make governments react. Is fear an effective method? Is fright any kind of weapon at all? What can terrorists hope to accomplish by sowing fear? How can it help their side to vanquish its opponents? Clearly it can do so in many ways. Fright can paralyze the will, befuddle the mind, and exhaust the strength of an adversary. Moreover, it can persuade an opponent that a particular political point of view is taken with such deadly seriousness by its few adherents that it should be accommodated, rather than suffering casualties year after year in a campaign to suppress it.

All of these elements came together, for example, in the struggle that led to the independence of southern Ireland. It is difficult to disentangle the role of terrorism in this achievement from the other elements that were involved, for the Irish also had put in motion what was, in effect, a guerrilla warfare campaign. Moreover, the Liberal members of the coalition that then governed the United Kingdom had a political commitment that went back more than a quarter of a century to the cause of Irish Home Rule. Yet there can be little doubt that terrorism played a major role in causing Britain to tire of the struggle.

Terrorism can also make heroes out of gunmen, and thereby rally popular support to their cause. The problem this creates for them is that when the time comes to make the compromises necessary in order to negotiate the terms of their victory, the glamour wanes, and with it, the political support. Michael Collins was a romantic figure who captured the imagination of all Ireland as long as he was an outlaw; but when he sat down to make peace, he was seen by many in a much different light. As he signed the Irish Treaty of 1921 on Britain's behalf, Lord Birkenhead remarked to Collins, "I may have signed my political death-warrant tonight"; to which Collins replied, "I may have signed my actual death-warrant." Eight months later Michael Collins lay dead on an Irish roadway with a bullet through his head.

Just as it can make gangsters into heroes, terrorist provocations can also make policemen into villains. The Black-and-Tans who fought the Irish revolutionists were, in an objective sense, so successful at repression that Michael Collins told an English official afterwards, in regard to the July 1921 peace negotiations: "You had us dead beat. We could not have lasted another three weeks." Yet Black-and-Tan methods made the cause of repression so odious that Britain was induced to choose another course of action.

Brutality is an induced governmental response that can

boomerang. It is this ability to use the strength of repression against itself, in many different ways, that has enabled terrorist strategies to succeed in many situations that have, rightly or wrongly, been described as colonialist in the modern world.

Tactics of the Irgun

Sophisticated approaches have been developed along these lines. One of these was explained to me and to others at a meeting in New York City sometime in 1945 by one of the founders of the Irgun Zvai Leumi, a tiny group of Jewish militants in what was then the British-mandated territory of Palestine. His organization had no more than 1,000 or 1,500 members, and it was at odds with the Palestinian Jewish community almost as much as it was with the mandatory regime. Yet he proposed to combat Great Britain, then a global power whose armed forces in the Second World War numbered in the millions, and to expel Great Britain from Palestine.

How could such a thousand-to-one struggle be won? To do so, as he explained it, his organization would attack property interests. After giving advance warning to evacuate them, his small band of followers would blow up buildings. This, he said, would lead the British to overreact by garrisoning the country with an immense army drawn from stations in other parts of the world. But postwar Britain could not afford financially to maintain so great an army either there or anywhere else for any extended period of time. Britain urgently needed to demobilize its armed forces. The strain would tell; and eventually economic pressure would drive the Attlee-Bevin government either to withdraw from Palestine or else to try some reckless and possibly losing gamble in an effort to retrieve the situation.

It can be argued that such is in fact what happened. Of course Britain might have withdrawn anyway, at some other time or for some other reason. But that is really beside the point, for the Irgun wanted independence then and there, in order to open up the country to refugees from Hitler's Europe. They got what they wanted when they wanted it by doing it in their own way.

There were two flaws in the Irgun strategy. It would have failed had the British not reacted to the destruction of buildings as they were expected to do. If instead they had done nothing at all, maintained only a modest military garrison, and sent for no reinforcements, all that would have happened would have been that a few more buildings would have been blown up and the owners would have collected the insurance money and would have rebuilt them; and the Irgun would have proved a failure.

In the second place, the plan of attacking property without hurting people proved to be unrealistic. Accidents inevitably occur when violence is unleashed. Almost a hundred persons were killed when the Irgun blew up the King David Hotel in Jerusalem. According to the plan, they should have been evacuated before the blast, but in actual life people misunderstand, or their telephone line is busy, or somebody forgets to give them the message in time. Moreover, terrorism generates its own momentum, and before long the killing becomes deliberate. The bloodshed caused by the Irgun isolated it politically and alienated the rest of the Palestinian Jewish community. The British failed to perceive or exploit this situation. But Ben-Gurion did; in 1948 he made use of it to crush the Irgun, for the Israeli army might have been unwilling to carry out orders to attack those unloading the Irgun ship the Altalena, if the Irgun had not used up its political credit before then by the taking of too many lives.

Yet despite its flaws, the strategy was sufficiently ingenious so that the Irgun played a big part in getting the British to withdraw. Its ingenuity lay in using an opponent's own strength against him. It was a sort of jujitsu. First the adversary was made to be afraid, and then, predictably, he would react to his fear by increasing the bulk of his strength, and then the sheer weight of that bulk would drag him down.

Another way of saying this is that the Irgun, seeing that it was too small to defeat Great Britain, decided, as an alternative approach, that Britain was big enough to defeat itself.

[Menahem Begin, Irgun leader and strategist, head of the opposition party in the Israeli parliament, became prime minister in June 1977.—Ed.]

Terror as Persuasion in Algeria

In the 1950s, the nationalist rebel group in Algeria developed yet another method of using the strength of an occupying power against itself. Their method was to induce that strength to be used as a form of persuasion.

For, in Algeria, the whole question was one of persuasion. The problem initially faced by the miniscule band of Algerian nationalists that called itself the National Liberation Front (or, in its French initials, FLN) was that Algeria at that time had little sense of national identity. Its population was not homogeneous; and the Berbers, the Arabs, and the settlers of European descent were peoples quite different from one another. The name and separate existence of Algeria were only of recent origin. For most of recorded history, Algeria had been no more than the middle part of North Africa, with no distinct history of its own. Legally it was merely the southern part of France. The French had treated Morocco and Tunisia as protectorates, with separate identities, but not Algeria, which was absorbed into France herself. With sarcasm, Frenchmen used to reply to Americans who urged independence for Algeria by saying that, on the same basis, the United States should set Wisconsin free or give back independence to South Carolina.

It was a jibe that went to the heart of the matter. Colonial empires were coming to an end in the 1950s and 1960s. If Algeria was a nation, then inevitably it would be set free to govern itself. Only if it were genuinely a part of France could it continue to be ruled from Paris. All depended, therefore, on whether the indigenous population could be convinced by the French government that Algeria was not a separate country, or upon whether they could be persuaded by the FLN to change their minds so as to think of themselves as a nation.

The FLN strategy of terrorism addressed itself to this central and decisive issue. By itself, as has been said, terror can accomplish nothing in terms of political goals; it can only aim at obtaining a response that will achieve those goals for it. What the FLN did was to goad the French into reacting in such a way as to demonstrate the unreality of the claim that there was no distinct Algerian nation. Unlike the Irgun, the FLN did not set out to campaign merely against property; it attacked people. It used random violence, planting bombs in market places and in other crowded locations. The instinctive French reaction was to treat all persons of non-European origin as suspects; but, as Raymond Aron was to write, "As suspects, all the Muslims felt excluded from the existing community." Their feeling was confirmed when, in the middle 1950s, the authorities further reacted by transferring the French army units composed of Muslim Algerian troops out of Algeria and into mainland France, and replacing them in Algeria by European troops. By such actions they showed in the most unmistakable way that they regarded no Algerians as Frenchmen except for the European settlers. They spoke of we and us, and of they and them, and did not realize that their doing so meant the end of *Algérie Française*.

Thus the French conceded the issue of the war at its very outset. They threw away the potential support of Muslim Algeria because they were skeptical of the possibility that it could be obtained. From that moment the conclusion of the conflict was foregone. Once the sympathies of the population had shifted to its side, the FLN was able to outgrow mere terrorism and to organize a campaign of guerrilla warfare. It also was enabled to appeal to world sympathies on behalf of a people fighting for its freedom. From the French point of view all had become hopeless; for no amount of force can keep an unwilling population indefinitely in subjection. Even though the FLN had written the script, the French, with suicidal logic, went ahead to play the role for which they had been cast.

The FLN success was therefore a special case. It required a particular kind of opponent. It could not be duplicated in other circumstances and conditions.

Recent Terrorist Tactics

Revolutionist-terrorists of the last decade have failed to perceive the special characteristics of the colonialist situation that facilitated success for Irish, Irgun, and Algerian terrorists. They have tried to apply the strategy of terrorism in situations that are essentially different. This has been true, for example, of extremist groups seeking to overthrow liberal-pluralistic regimes during the 1960s. Their theory has been that their terrorist attacks would force hitherto liberal regimes to become repressive, a change which in turn would alienate the masses, thus setting the stage for revolution. But it has not worked out that way in practice. In the United States, for example, terrorist bomb attacks have not led to any change at all in the form of government, much less to a transformation of America into a police state. On the other hand, in Uruguay, once the model democracy of Latin America, the terror of the Tupamaro bands has led to a military dictatorship that brutally destroyed the Tupamaros, but that does not seem, at least as yet, to have led to the predicted reaction by the masses in favor of revolutionary action.

Other revolutionary groups have taken a somewhat different approach. They have argued that liberal democracies are already police states. Thus, the object of revolutionary terrorist action should be to reveal this hidden reality to the population at large. Unthinking reaction by the authorities to terrorist provocation would accomplish the desired result. Thus the aim of terrorism would be to trick the government into taking off its mask.

In open societies such as Great Britain and the United States, the liberal democratic features have proved to be a face and not a mask: there is nothing to take off, and the strategy failed because its factual premise proved to be untrue.

In closed societies, the strategy has been to show that authoritarian regimes are actually impotent despite their outward show of virility. In such circumstances, supposedly, by demonstrating that the public authorities are powerless to enforce law and order, a campaign of terror can cause a government to collapse; but the flaw in the theory is that the terrorists usually are not strong enough to take its place. Either some more broadly based group will seize power, or else, as in Argentina, private groups will take the law into their own hands and retaliate in kind against murder and extortion, so that society relapses into a semi-anarchic state of reprisals and blood feuds, where terrorists are buried with their victims.

Publicity by Terror

It is against this background that Arab Palestinian terrorism has seized the attention of the contemporary world. It is aimed at Israel; it is aimed at the Arabs who live within Israel; and it is aimed at the world outside. It is, in other words, a mixed strategy. Each of its mixed aspects has to be considered separately. All that Arab terrorism can accomplish in the land that has been promised to so many is to frighten and to threaten the Arab inhabitants of Israel in order to keep them from cooperating with the Israeli authorities. Israel itself, however, cannot be terrorized into disappearing of its own accord; yet removing Israel from the map has long been the proclaimed goal of the Arab terrorist movement.

Terrorism can be employed more successfully in colonialist situations than in Palestine because a colonial power suffers the disadvantage of fighting the battle away from its own base, and also because a colonial power, having a country of its own to which it can withdraw, is under no compulsion to fight to the bitter end. The Israelis, though termed colonialist by the Arabs, are fighting on home terri-

tory, and they have no other country to which they can
withdraw; they fight with their backs to the sea. They can
be goaded into a self-defeating reaction, but unless they
permit that to happen, nothing can be done to their domestic public opinion that is likely to destroy them. The Arab
terrorists therefore have turned elsewhere, and have attacked the arteries of world transportation in hopes that a
world indifferent to the merits of the Arab-Israeli dispute
will turn against the Israelis in order to end the annoyance
of a disrupted airline service.

In doing so they have strayed across a frontier and into
the eerie world of Mr. McLuhan [Marshall McLuhan, the
communications expert], and they have transformed terrorism into a form of mass communication—but communication aimed at the whole world and not, as in the case of
Algeria, mostly at the indigenous population. Theirs is a
campaign that needs publicity in order to succeed, and
therefore they have come to operate within the ambit of
contemporary public relations and communications arts:
the world of cinema, camp fashion, and pop art, in which
deadlines and prime-time are the chief realities and in
which shock value is the chief virtue. If audiences throughout the world react with horror, and turn against the political cause in whose name so many innocent people have been
harmed and killed, the strategy will have backfired. So far
they have not done so and it has not done so.

It is a corruption of the human spirit for which all
political sides are responsible. The left-wing journalist Paul
Johnson wrote an article some months back arguing that
left-wing movements are as much at fault as anybody else
for accepting the murder of the innocent as a legitimate
means for the pursuit of political ends. He quoted the six-
teenth century humanist Castellio, "who was lucky to
escape burning by both Catholics and Protestants, and who
pointed out in his tract for toleration, *Whether Heretics
Are to Be Persecuted?*, that no certitude of righteousness
justifies violence: 'To kill a man is not to defend a doctrine,

it is to kill a man.' " Appalled at the welcome accorded by the United Nations to the leader of the Arab terrorists, Johnson wrote that, "Step by step, almost imperceptibly, without anyone being aware that a fatal watershed has been crossed, mankind has descended into the age of terror."

The Strategy of Terrorism

If this is an age of terror, then it has become all the more important for us to understand exactly what it is that terrorism means. Terrorism, as has been seen, is the weapon of those who are prepared to use violence but who believe that they would lose any contest of sheer strength. All too little understood, the uniqueness of the strategy lies in this: that it achieves its goal not through its acts but through the response to its acts. In any other such strategy, the violence is the beginning and its consequences are the end of it. For terrorism, however, the consequences of the violence are themselves merely a first step and form a stepping stone toward objectives that are more remote. Whereas military and revolutionary actions aim at a physical result, terrorist actions aim at a psychological result.

But even that psychological result is not the final goal. Terrorism is violence used in order to create fear; but it is aimed at creating fear in order that the fear, in turn, will lead somebody else—not the terrorist—to embark on some quite different program of action that will accomplish whatever it is that the terrorist really desires. Unlike the soldier, the guerrilla fighter, or the revolutionist, the terrorist therefore is always in the paradoxical position of undertaking actions the immediate physical consequences of which are not particularly desired by him. An ordinary murderer will kill somebody because he wants the person to be dead, but a terrorist will shoot somebody even though it is a matter of complete indifference to him whether that person lives or dies. He would do so, for example, in order to provoke a brutal police repression that he believes will lead to political conditions propitious to revolutionary agitation and

organization aimed at overthrowing the government. The
act of murder is the same in both cases, but its purpose is
different, and each act plays a different role in the strategies
of violence.

Only an understanding of the purpose for which such an
act is undertaken can enable us to know the nature of the
act. When Julius Caesar was murdered in the Roman Senate, it was an assassination of the traditional sort, intended
to eliminate a specific figure from the political scene; but
had he been killed there by the representative of a subversive sect, intent on plunging his dagger into the first Roman
leader he encountered in order to provoke a certain political
response from the Senate, it would instead have been an act
of political terrorism.

It is because an action of the same sort may be undertaken by two different groups with two quite different ends
in view that terrorism is so often confused with guerrilla
warfare, for terrorists and guerrillas often seem to be doing
the same sorts of things. Both of them, for example, often
sabotage transportation facilities. When T. E. Lawrence
led his classic guerrilla warfare campaign against Turkish
rule in Arabia, he systematically dynamited railway tracks
and bridges. Lawrence's strategy was later explained by
Winston Churchill as follows: "The Turkish armies operating against Egypt depended upon the desert railway. This
slender steel track ran through hundreds of miles of blis-
tering desert. If it were permanently cut the Turkish armies
must perish." And Lawrence therefore rode on camelback
across the sands to destroy the enemy army by blowing up
its transportation facilities. In recent years those who say
that they wish to destroy the state of Israel have also blown
up transportation facilities in the Arab desert; in this case,
jet airplanes belonging to civil aviation companies. Yet if
thereby they were to permanently cut the airline networks
of TWA or BOAC they would not cause the Israeli army to
perish. Indeed the fate of such civil aviation companies is
a matter of indifference to the terrorists. Lawrence the guer-

rilla leader attacked a railway because he wanted to destroy it, whereas Arab terrorists attack an airline even though they do not want to destroy it.

The distinction is of more than academic importance. The French lost their empire over Algeria when they mistook terrorism for guerrilla warfare. They thought that when the FLN planted a bomb in a public bus, it was in order to blow up the bus; whereas the real FLN purpose in planting the bomb was not to blow up the bus, but to lure authorities into reacting by arresting all the non-Europeans in the area as suspects.

Vulnerabilities of the Terrorist

The terrorist is like a magician who tricks you into watching his right hand while his left hand, unnoticed, makes the switch. It is understandable that the French authorities in Algeria became totally obsessed by the need to stamp out criminal attacks, but it was fatal to their policy to do so, for the violent attacks were merely a subsidiary issue. The tiny FLN band of outlaws could have blown up every bus in all of Algeria and never won a convert to their cause of independence. Failing to understand the strategy of terrorism, the French did not see that it was not the FLN's move, but rather the French countermove, that would determine whether the FLN succeeded or failed.

It may be the case that the current Israeli policy of attacking Arab terrorist bases in southern Lebanon is another example of concentrating too much attention on preventing terrorist actions and too little attention on foiling terrorist purposes. The Israeli policy is certainly understandable on many grounds, and valid arguments can be adduced in its support; but the weakening of an essentially benevolent Lebanese government, as well as the further estrangement of world opinion, are results of the Israeli raids into Lebanon that may outweigh the value of using that particular approach to the problem of combating terrorism.

For the Israelis, threatened by enemies outside of their

society, the problem is an enormously difficult one. For societies threatened only by enemies from within, it is considerably less so. The very wickedness of terrorism makes it a vulnerable strategy in such a society. Other strategies sometimes kill the innocent by mistake. Terrorism kills the innocent deliberately; for not even the terrorist necessarily believes that the particular person who happens to become his victim deserves to be killed or injured. It is horrifying not merely because of the deed that is done but also because at first the deed seems pointless. If you want to make war on the United States on behalf of Puerto Rican independence, why blow up a historic tavern in New York's financial district? What has Fraunces Tavern got to do with Puerto Rico? Why not attack the alleged forces of occupation in Puerto Rico instead? If you opposed by force and violence the continuation of US aid to South Vietnam, why threaten to destroy the Smithsonian Institution? What had its plant collections and its ichthyological specimens to do with American policy in Southeast Asia? The destruction seems so purposeless that it is a natural reaction to turn on those who perpetrate it in hatred and in anger.

The tragedies that befall great public figures can sometimes seem to have been deserved; but when a man on the street is killed at random on behalf of a cause with which he had nothing to do, it is a different matter and provokes a different reaction. In a homogeneous society, at any rate, it leads to a reaction against the terrorism, and it renders it vulnerable to a campaign that politically isolates it in order to physically destroy it, for the nature of the attacks tends to demonstrate that terrorists are enemies of the people rather than merely of the government. It is for this reason that Che Guevara, as a theoretician and practitioner of guerrilla warfare, warned against the strategy of terrorism, arguing that it hinders "contact with the masses and makes impossible unification for actions that will be necessary at a critical moment."

Even in the international arena, terrorist movements are

vulnerable when their actions alienate support. This was
tacitly recognized by the Palestine Liberation Organization
(PLO) when on January 29, 1975, it announced that hence-
forth it had decided to treat hijacking of airplanes, ships,
or trains as crimes and would impose death penalties on
hijackers if their actions led to the loss of life. Whether the
PLO will indeed abandon its campaign of terror against
international transportation remains to be seen. Yet the
declaration of its intention to do so is in itself significant,
for it suggests a realization that a point has arrived when a
public identification with terrorist activity will harm rather
than help. This is because terrorism is so much more evil
than other strategies of violence that public opinion sometimes can be rallied against it.

The Weakness of Preventive Measures

Indeed, in view of its inherent weakness, it is remark-
able how many political successes have been scored by the
strategy of terrorism in the last few decades. Its success
seems to be due in large part to a miscomprehension of the
strategy by its opponents. They have neglected the more
important of the two levels on which terrorism operates.
They have failed to focus on the crucial issue of how the
manner in which they, as opponents, respond affects the
political goals of the terrorists. Discussion instead has cen-
tered on the criminal justice aspects of the question: prevention and punishment.

Much has been written, for example, about the technological defenses that have been developed or could be
developed against terrorism in order to prevent it from
occurring. This can be a highly useful line of approach, as
the successful use of electronic surveillance devices at airports seems to have demonstrated. It may even be advisable
to require that any new technologies that are developed
from time to time should incorporate some sort of internal
defense against attack, much as environmentalists argue
that pollution control devices should be incorporated in

equipment and its cost charged to the manufacturers. Yet no technology is perfect, and there will always be somebody who will manage to slip by any defenses that can be created.

Prevention of terrorism in non-technological ways scarcely merits discussion. Perhaps one day the social sciences will teach us how to drain the swamps of misery in which hatred and fanaticism breed, but at the moment that day seems far distant. The hollow formalism of the law offers, if anything, even less help. Ingenious schemes for new international tribunals and procedures have been proposed, and they completely miss the point. The manifest unwillingness of many governments to use existing legal remedies against terrorism shows that the real problem is the lack of a will and not the lack of a way. For example, it was only when an attack was staged at the Paris airport that the French minister of the interior, in January of 1975, proposed to negotiate an international convention to provide for the punishment of terrorist acts. It is not any kind of genuine solution, in any event, but it will be interesting to see if Michel Poniatowski perseveres in even so ritualistic a response as this after the fleeting memory of injured national pride fades from view. There are all too many who object to terrorism only when they are its victims.

Far more effective than the reaction of M. Poniatowski was that of the French press. There were suggestions in the newspapers that the pro-Arab policy of the French government should be reversed because it had failed to prevent the attack at Orly airport. Within days the Palestine Liberation Organization strongly condemned the attack. It also announced that it had taken measures to punish persons who engaged in the hijacking of airplanes, boats or trains. What the French journalists had correctly intuited was that the locus of the struggle was not at the Orly airport: it was at the Elysée Palace and at the Quai d'Orsay. [The Elysée Palace is the residence of the president of the Republic of France; the Quai d'Orsay, the location of the Foreign Office.—Ed.]

The overriding questions are not legal or technological;

they are philosophical and political. Terrorism is the indirect strategy that wins or loses only in terms of how you respond to it. The decision as to how accommodating or how uncompromising you should be in your response to it involves questions that fall primarily within the domain of political philosophy.

The Choice for Society

Those who are the targets of terrorism—and who are prepared to defend themselves by doing whatever is necessary in order to beat it—start with a major advantage. The advantage is that success or failure depends upon them alone. Terrorism wins only if you respond to it in the way that the terrorists want you to; which means that its fate is in your hands and not in theirs. If you choose not to respond at all, or else to respond in a way different from that which they desire, they will fail to achieve their objectives.

The important point is that the choice is yours. That is the ultimate weakness of terrorism as a strategy. It means that, though terrorism cannot always be prevented, it can always be defeated. You can always refuse to do what they want you to do.

Whether to pay the price of defeating terrorism is increasingly going to be a major question in our time. The answer is relatively easy in most kidnapping and ransom situations: experience has shown that blackmailers and extortionists usually are encouraged to try it again if you give in to their demands the first time. So, if you can do so, you should accept the consequences, however terrible, of standing firm in order to avoid an infinite sequence of painful events.

But the price of doing so is constantly rising, as technology increases the range and magnitude of horrible possibilities. Terrorist outrages, when they occur, are bound to become more deadly. Increasingly, we will be under pressure to abridge our laws and liberties in order to suppress the terrorists. It is a pressure that should be resisted.

In our personal lives we sometimes have to choose be-

tween these alternatives: whether to live a good life or
whether to live a long life. Political society in the years to
come is likely to face a similar choice. An open society such
as ours is especially vulnerable to terrorist violence, which
seems to threaten us with ever more dreadful and drastic
fates. Have we the stoicism to endure nonetheless? Will we
be tempted to abandon our political and moral values? Will
we be willing to go on paying an ever higher price in order
to defeat the terrorists by refusing to respond in the way they
want us to?

Of course it would make things easier if terrorism simply
would go away. It seems unlikely to do so. The weapons are
at hand, and they probably will be used, for terrorism will
never cease until the day when the Old Man of the Moun-
tain loses his last disciple. The old man was grand master
of the sect called the Assassins (hashish-ins) because of the
hashish which he gave them. [The sect existed in the Middle
East in the 11th century.—Ed.] The old man, according to
Marco Polo, used to drug his young disciples and transport
them while they were asleep to his secret pleasure garden,
persuading them when they awoke in it that it was paradise
itself. Drugging them again, he would transport them back
to the everyday world while they slept. Never afterward did
they doubt that their Master could and would reward them
with eternal paradise after death if they did his killing for
him while they were alive. And so they did do his killing
for him.

If anything, the modern world seems to breed more and
more votaries of this peculiar sect. They seem to thrive and
multiply everywhere in the world, bomb or machine gun in
hand, motivated by political fantasies and hallucinations,
fully convinced that their slaughter of the innocent will
somehow usher in a political millennium for mankind.
"Voici le temps des Assassins," as Rimbaud [French poet of
the latter half of the 19th century] wrote in the dawn of the
industrial age; and we do indeed live in the time of the
Assassins.

THE UPSURGE IN TERROR [2]

One morning in September 1974, fifteen terrorists dressed as police and telephone repairmen blockaded a limousine in Buenos Aires traffic. They coldly executed the chauffeur and a front-seat passenger, who was the manager of Argentina's largest corporation, Bunge & Born, as they stood with their hands in the air. The terrorists then spirited off the company's owner-executives, Jorge and Juan Born.

Last June [1975], full-page advertisements in the Washington *Post* and four European newspapers announced that the kidnappers, members of the *Montoneros* movement, had "tried" the Born brothers and found them guilty of crimes of "exploitation" committed by their "multi-national monopoly." Upon payment of a ransom of $60 million, plus distribution of $1 million in merchandise to villages, factories, schools and hospitals, the Born brothers were freed.

Such kidnapping and violence, for ransom or for political blackmail, have become a major "growth industry."

☐ In September 1974, Japanese terrorists stormed the French embassy at The Hague. They held the ambassador and ten others hostage. Finally, the French government delivered an imprisoned terrorist comrade; the Dutch paid a $300,000 ransom and flew the group to Syria.

☐ The world got a further chilling look at these globe-hopping Japanese fanatics early . . . [in] August [1975], when five of them took over the US embassy building in Kuala Lumpur, Malaysia, and held fifty-one persons hostage, threatening to blow up the building unless seven of their comrades were released from prison in Japan. Three days later, after intensive negotiations to find a country

[2] From "Terrorism on the Rampage," by Robert S. Strother, roving editor, and Eugene H. Methvin, senior editor, of *Reader's Digest. Reader's Digest.* 107:73-7. N. '75. Reprinted with permission from the November 1975 *Reader's Digest.* Copyright 1975 by The Reader's Digest Assn., Inc. R. S. Strother is also a veteran foreign correspondent; E. H. Methvin, a recognized authority on terrorism, author of *The Riot Makers.*

willing to give them asylum, the terrorists were flown by
Japan Air Lines to Libya.

☐ Last February [1975], West Germany's Red Army Group
kidnapped a leading mayoral candidate on election eve in
West Berlin. Their demand of the West German government: free six imprisoned comrades and pay $50,000 ransom.
For seventy-two hours, the terrorists controlled West Germany's national TV network; news coverage had to include
statements dictated by the freed comrades, who were flown
to South Yemen.

☐ Two months later, six other German terrorists seized
West Germany's embassy in Stockholm, killing one person.
This time, the Bonn government rejected the demand for
ransom—$500,000—and freedom for twenty-six prisoners.
After murdering one of their twelve hostages, the raiders
blew up the embassy and tried to escape. Five were rounded
up; a sixth committed suicide.

☐ In October 1974 in New York City, five simultaneous
bombings marked the resumption of Puerto Rican terrorist
actions, which have involved more than one hundred bombs
in department stores and other buildings since 1969. Last
January [1975] during a busy noon hour, a time bomb killed
four and injured more than fifty at Fraunces Tavern, Man-
hattan's oldest building, in the financial district. A note proclaimed that the attack was aimed at "reactionary corporate
executives inside." At the core of the campaign, say intelligence specialists, are 135 Puerto Ricans trained in Cuba for
sabotage, armed robbery, kidnapping and assassination.

Epidemic

Today's epidemic of savagery began with the kidnap-
murder of US ambassador John G. Mein by Cuba-aided
Guatemala terrorists in 1968. Since then, 82 US diplomats
and other officials abroad have been attacked—33 of them
kidnapped, 18 murdered and 31 wounded; British, Canadian, Japanese, French and West German ambassadors have
suffered similar attacks.

At home, the FBI has recorded 688 incidents of terrorist violence in the last four and one half years—ranging from bombings and ambush-murders to bank robberies, arson and sniping. Eighty-three police and civilians died and 284 were wounded in these episodes. The FBI has identified 21 terrorist groups, embracing an estimated 5,000 members and auxiliaries, who are building clandestine networks to attack our society. The Weather Underground, which boasts of bombing the US Capitol, Pentagon, State Department and a score of other targets coast-to-coast, is publicly advertising that it will "bring the fireworks" to the nation's 1976 Bicentennial celebration. [See Terrorism in the United States" in Section II, below.]

What's behind the global upsurge? Who are the perpetrators, and what motivates them? Many factors, all stemming from new developments which are revolutionizing human society everywhere, contribute:

☐ New technology enables tiny groups to wield unprecedented powers of destruction. For example, on September 5, 1973, Italian police arrested five Arabs in an apartment near Rome's International Airport. Those apprehended were terrorists preparing to shoot down an Israeli airliner. Their weapons were two Soviet SA-7 heat-seeking missiles, each to be fired from a light shoulder launcher.

☐ Modern global television offers a tempting, instantaneous audience of millions, as the Arab terrorists so dramatically demonstrated by capturing Israeli athletes at the 1972 Munich Olympics—an episode which ended in the shootout deaths of eleven Israelis, five terrorists, one policeman. (And, of course, television itself, by providing instant and graphic communication, helps to spread ideas and foster imitation.) [See "Gaining the Media's Attention" in Section III, below.]

☐ The post–World War II population explosion is dumping onto the economies of the United States and underdeveloped nations alike millions of restless, underemployed youths ready to blame "the system" for their rootless, un-used lives. Typically, in Sri Lanka (formerly called Ceylon), thousands of college-educated but jobless youths went on a Maoist-inspired rampage in 1971. Young people in Latin America and Africa, without work or limited to menial tasks, are similarly vulnerable to the call of charismatic guer-rilla leaders.

Who, by and large, are behind this war on society? Ac-cording to crime experts and behavioral scientists, there are three main categories of terrorists, although the dividing lines are usually blurred:

1. *Rootless Rebels.* Uruguayan terrorists kidnapped British ambassador Geoffrey Jackson in January 1971, and held him prisoner in a two-by-six-foot cage for eight months. "Most of my captors were students, and many were quite abnormal," wrote Jackson. "Ferocity, far more than precise ideology, was the main single and common component of their assorted personalities."

Whether they come from the United States, Quebec, Japan, Latin America, Europe or the Middle East, these rebels invariably bear the "true believer" stamp. Theirs is a fairy-tale ideological world of good guys versus bad guys.

Says Montreal psychiatrist Dr. Gustave Morf, who stud-ied in depth many of the dozens of Quebec terrorists con-victed in the 1960s wave of bombings, killings and armed robberies: "The conspirators felt they were living a life of adventure, reminiscent of the high-seas pirates described in books. It seems that the liberation of Quebec had been only a pretext to give free rein to those romantic criminal tenden-cies which may lurk in many people. A growing number of adolescents refuse to grow up, to take responsibility. Many become eternal students, reaching age thirty or forty without having held a responsible job."

Soviet terror schools teach their agents to exploit such social and economic dropouts. One recruit, who later de-fected, was told:

Go search for people who are hurt by fate or nature—the ugly, those suffering from an inferiority complex, craving power and influence, but defeated by unfavorable circumstances. For the first time in their lives they will experience a sense of importance.

2. *Minorities.* Many rootless rebels, goaded by an outraged sense of injustice, come from ethnic and national minorities—America's urban black youth, the Quebec French and the Palestinian refugees, for example. Deprived of cultural or national identity, they latch onto the revolutionary role-model offered in extremist propaganda.

A young Palestinian, Fawaz Turki, in his book *The Disinherited* [Monthly Review Press] (1972), explained the process:

I hated the world and the order of reality around me. I hated being dispossessed of a nation and an identity. I hated being a hybrid, an outcast, a zero. Give me a gun, man, and I will blow my own or somebody else's brains out.

Such men make ready recruits for ideologies promising salvation through violence.

3. *Criminals.* Common bandits, quick to exploit profitable tactics, may follow the terrorists' lead toward kidnapping and blackmail. In Mexico, Colombia and Brazil, gangs of extortionists, robbers and kidnappers frequently have posed as political terrorists, adopting revolutionary slogans and rationales for their convenience. And terrorists often hire criminal types, to exploit their skills and anti-social drives.

Counteraction

How can we defend ourselves?

The United States has already taken many effective steps. The government has tightened airport security, increased scrutiny of foreign travelers, coached American businessmen working abroad, and improved protection of our diplomats. Washington advertises a tough policy of no ransom or release of prisoners in return for hostages. Explains [former] Secretary of State Henry Kissinger:

> If terrorist groups get the impression they can force a negotiation with the United States and acquiescence in their demands, we may save lives in one place at the risk of hundreds everywhere else.

But international counteraction has proved disappointing. In 1972, the United Nations General Assembly Legal Committee turned down a tough American proposal which recommended that member nations return terrorist criminals for trial in the country of their crime. Instead, the committee voted 76–34 in favor of a "do-nothing" study. To top that off, the Assembly invited and treated as a head of state Yasir Arafat, leader of the most formidable Palestinian terrorist group. [See "Can the UN Act?" in Section V, below.]

Clearly, the advanced nations which are prime targets of the terrorists must proceed, jointly or unilaterally, to apply to nations harboring and otherwise encouraging terrorist operations such sanctions as cutting off airline service, stopping mail and telecommunications and international food and financial help.

Any effective counteraction must not only catch bombers and kidnappers, but uncover and smash their elaborate support auxiliaries as well. Ultimately, then, the only truly effective counter-weapon is *intelligence*. That means—in the United States—giving the FBI the legal and scientific tools it needs, plus public understanding and support for their aggressive use. It means spies, networks of paid informers, wiretaps, bugs, computerized dossier systems—the whole spectrum of clandestine warfare so necessary to the cause, yet so vulnerable to attack by civil-libertarian extremists.

Congress should immediately authorize the FBI to use wiretaps and bugs—forbidden at present—for anti-terrorist intelligence collection. Such safeguards as requiring the Attorney General personally to approve and report his actions annually in secret to bipartisan congressional committees can deter capers such as the Nixon Administration's Watergate break-in. Truly, as a British Privy Council Committee on wiretapping declared in 1957,

> The freedom of the individual is quite valueless if he can be made the victim of the lawbreaker. If these powers are properly and wisely exercised, they are in themselves aids to the maintenance of the true freedom of the individual.

From Moscow, before his banishment, Aleksandr Solzhenitsyn reminded the world:

> Hijackings and all other forms of terrorism have been spreading tenfold precisely because everyone is ready to capitulate before them. But as soon as some firmness is shown, terrorism can be smashed forever. We will have to erase from human consciousness the very idea that anyone has the right to use force against justice, law and mutual consent.

THE NEW "THEATER OF FEAR" [3]

Before [December 1975], how many people had ever heard of the islands of Molucca? Probably not many. But a handful of militant Moluccan youths in the Netherlands have changed all that.

They seized first a train, then a consulate. They demanded that the case for an independent South Molucca be heard. To give brute force to their words, they murdered several of the many hostages they had taken.

The world looked on aghast. Through millions of television sets, radios, and newspapers it suddenly became aware of the Moluccan "cause" and of the 35,000-member Moluccan community in the Netherlands, exiles from the Pacific islands that once were Dutch and now are part of Indonesia. [For a more detailed account of this episode, see "Incident in Holland" in Section II, below.—Ed.]

[3] From "Coming to Grips With World Terrorism," by David Anable, staff correspondent. *Christian Science Monitor.* p 3. D. 19, '75. Reprinted by permission from *The Christian Science Monitor.* © 1975 The Christian Science Publishing Society. All rights reserved.

Here was a terrible but classic case of international terrorism, a problem the world has yet to come to grips with. According to specialists in the field, terrorism is the "weapon of the weak." It is psychological warfare. Incidents that directly affect only a small number of people are given enormous mental impact by the perverse but skilled use of violence and horror, whose shock waves then buffet millions. In that sense at least, say the experts, terrorism "works."

According to one leading specialist in international terrorism, Brian Jenkins of the Rand Corporation, there were some seven hundred incidents of international terrorism between 1968 and mid-1975. In all, about seven hundred people lost their lives and seventeen hundred were wounded or injured. (For these purposes "international terrorism" is defined as terrorists operating outside their own country, that is, incidents involving more than one country.)

This toll, Dr. Jenkins points out, is dwarfed by the fighting in Northern Ireland or Lebanon. It is almost "trivial" compared with the losses in an industrial society from accidents and crime. . . . [In 1975] alone, for instance, the American murder rate topped 20,000.

The total dollar loss, Dr. Jenkins adds, "in terms of planes blown up and ransom payments is less than the annual loss in this country from shoplifting."

The overwhelming problem, however, is that the consequences of these comparatively isolated acts are anything but trivial. They prompt enormously costly and sometimes disruptive security precautions. In some countries they lead to repressive retaliation and erosion of civil liberties. They can even present a basic challenge to the accepted international system of states.

"It's dramatic violence; it's almost choreographed violence, theatrical violence, carried out for its psychological effect on the people watching," says Dr. Jenkins. "It is designed to create fear, which makes people exaggerate the terrorists and the strength of their cause."

The world has been caught off-balance by this evolving

form of psychological warfare. It has been able to reach agreement on combating only a few specific aspects of international terrorism, hijacking aircraft and protecting diplomats. Even these agreements became possible only after terrorist activities soared to such a peak that they could no longer be ignored.

Hijacking, for instance, occurred quite often in the 1950s. But then it was largely a matter of East Europeans seizing planes to break through the Iron Curtain. On arrival in the West they tended to be hailed as heroes.

It was not until hijacking became far more pervasive and violent in the 1960s that worldwide pressure for action began to grow. Finally, after a spate of dramatic Palestinian hijackings, the International Civil Aviation Organization (ICAO, a Montreal-based UN affiliate) succeeded in drafting a couple of anti-hijack conventions.

International Agreements

One, against hijacking in the air, was adopted in 1970. The other, to outlaw attacks on aircraft on the ground, was voted through in 1971. Both were subsequently ratified and are in force.

By the time these conventions took effect, however, hijacking was very much on the wane for a variety of other reasons.

The anti-hijack precautions of individual countries had become intense. The United States had concluded a bilateral treaty with Cuba providing for the prosecution or return of hijackers and the return of hijacked airliners, their passengers and crews, and any funds extorted. [This agreement expired early in 1977.—Ed.]

A growing number of other countries, from Kuwait to Algeria, were becoming disenchanted with their role as hijackers' havens. And perhaps most significant, the Palestine Liberation Organization had decided that such indiscriminate tactics were becoming politically counterproductive.

As hijacking diminished a new phase emerged: the kidnap and murder of diplomats. Since virtually all nations have vested interest in the safety of their own diplomats, agreement on outlawing this variety of terrorism was fairly quickly reached. In December 1973, the United Nations passed the necessary convention. It will come into force when ratified by 22 countries; so far 11 have done so. [The convention came into force February 20, 1977. Subsequently three more nations ratified it.—Ed.]

But the broader, overall problem of international terrorism remains unsolved. There is not even a universal desire to tackle it, let alone a consensus on how that might be done.

The nub of the deadlock is that one person's "terrorist" is another person's "freedom fighter." Those who want to retain the international status quo, and those who burn to change it, have totally conflicting viewpoints. One side condemns group or individual "terrorism"; the other side rages against national "terrorism" or repression.

PLO as Key Example

The Palestine Liberation Organization (PLO) is a key example.

Most Arabs see the PLO as the heroic fighter for the Palestinian national cause. It is bracketed with the African and other liberation movements that struggled against European colonialism.

Not surprisingly, Israelis have a different point of view. In the words of Israel's Ambassador to the UN, Chaim Herzog, the PLO is "a coterie of feuding terrorist gangs" intent on Israel's destruction.

The other nations of the world take sides according to a motley array of motives: their sympathy with the Palestinian or Israeli cause; their own suffering from PLO terrorism; their degree of dependence on Arab oil.

To a lesser degree, much the same divisions arise over most other politically motivated terrorism. Hence the near impossibility of reaching an international consensus on any broad assault on the problem.

. . . [In] August [1975], for instance, United States Secretary of State Henry A. Kissinger in a speech in Montreal urged the United Nations to take up an American anti-terrorism proposal: a convention to combat a wide range of international terrorist methods including kidnapping, murder, and "other brutal acts." But subsequent American soundings here indicate clearly that opposition to such a move is just as great now as ever.

This was vividly illustrated . . . [in December 1975]: The headlines were filled with news of terrorist attacks and of the plight of hostages. In the Netherlands it was the Moluccans; in London a couple were held in their own living room by fleeing gunmen of the Irish Republican Army; in Ethiopia four Americans, a Briton, an Italian, and several Chinese were kept captive by Eritrean separatists; in Beirut two other abducted Americans were still missing; in Chad a lonely Frenchwoman endured her nineteenth month in the hands of rebel tribesmen.

Meanwhile, back at the UN, the General Assembly quietly shelved the whole issue of terrorism for yet another year. The item has been on the agenda ever since the 1972 Munich Olympics massacre of Israeli athletes—and at each session it has been briskly swept back under the UN carpet.

The Mideast cycle of violence, too, was raised another callous notch. In November a bomb explosion in Jerusalem had killed seven people. In December Israeli air strikes into Lebanon, officially aimed at alleged terrorist concentrations, killed some one hundred people, including women and children.

A fruitless UN Security Council debate quickly followed. Once again it reflected the customary divisions over state (Israeli) versus group (PLO) recourse to violence.

This international failure has compelled individual countries to take their own precautions. Following the 1972 Munich massacre the American Administration set up a special Cabinet committee. This, in turn, appointed a working group under a special assistant to the Secretary of State. The group, with members from more than twenty government departments, still meets every other week to coordinate US anti-terrorist activities and to commission and sift research. [For more detailed information on this interagency group see "International Terrorism: A Survey," by R. A. Fearey in Section II, below and "American Policy Against Terrorism," by Lewis Hoffacker, in Section IV, below.—Ed.]

The dangers of the world's failure to confront international terrorism remain. According to American experts, failure to condemn terrorist methods confers a certain "respectability" on them. Worse, they say, success with today's methods provides an incentive to escalate to even more extravagant forms of violence.

The Italian police, they point out, only just succeeded in preventing Arab terrorists near the Rome airport from firing heat-seeking missiles at an airliner in 1973. Carefully researched, but little publicized, is the possibility of terrorists gaining access to nuclear or chemical or biological weapons. [See "The Ever-Violent Middle East" in Section II, below.]

"We are coping with people who lack the resources to deal in more conventional forms of war," says Dr. Jenkins.

Instead they deal in the theater of fear. We are all the audience.

SIZING UP THE MENACE [4]

Reprinted from *U.S. News & World Report.*

Mr. Fearey, are we going to see more and more terrorism all over the world?

Terrorism seems likely to be a growing, increasingly important and increasingly dangerous thing in the years ahead.

---

[4] From "Terrorism: 'Growing and Increasingly Dangerous,'" interview with Robert A. Fearey, former special assistant to the Secretary of State and Coordinator for Combatting Terrorism. *U.S. News & World Report.* 79:77-9. S. 29, '75.

On the other hand, we can't be sure. Remember all the turmoil at our universities in the late sixties? We began to wonder whether they were ever going to be able to operate again. Then that died out.

Haven't terrorists been pretty successful lately?

Terrorists have had some tactical successes, but I don't think they've been successful in achieving their political purposes. Quite the contrary, terrorist organizations are arousing increasing revulsion.

If terrorism fails in its basic purposes—which are fundamentally political—in enough instances over a period of time, then it could go out of fashion and become a declining problem.

But when you look around the world you see hundreds of millions of deprived and frustrated peoples who are now well aware that there is a better life. They hear and see it through the media, while their own lot is often getting worse. In these circumstances, terrorism—the resort of the weak—may have increasing appeal.

However, we should not give terrorists too much credit for sincere political belief.

Many are ordinary criminals using political arguments to rationalize their crimes. And political grievances, no matter how strongly felt, cannot justify the murder of innocent people.

Do terrorists have trouble getting weapons?

No—and new types of weapons are constantly adding to terrorists' capabilities. All sorts of small, portable, easy-to-operate, highly accurate and highly destructive weapons are being adopted by armed forces, with constant danger of their falling into the hands of terrorists.

The classic example is the SA-7—the Soviet portable, heat-seeking rocket with which one man could bring down a 747 jet. SA-7 rockets, similar to our Redeye, were found in the hands of Palestinian terrorists—just in time—at the Rome airport in 1973.

Moreover, modern complex and interdependent societies present a plethora of targets for terrorists, not limited to aircraft. There's even concern that, at some point, terrorists might try using weapons of mass destruction.

Do you mean nuclear weapons?

We've had threats of this sort already, though none were anything more than hoaxes. There's no evidence they ever came close to possessing nuclear weapons.

How about homemade chemical and biological weapons —poisoning of water systems, that sort of operation?

Yes—the possibility of terrorist threats based on such things exists. If one lets one's imagination run, a number of frightening opportunities for terrorists suggest themselves.

Are you concerned about a possible alliance of governments with terrorists?

Well, you have the possibility of aggressor governments concluding that modern warfare is too expensive, too destructive and too risky. They might turn instead to surrogate terrorist techniques where they would, in effect, employ a terrorist organization to go into a target country and disrupt and subvert it.

The cost to the aggressor would be very low; it could deny any connection with the enterprise, and the results achieved in the target state could be fully as effective if not more effective, than through overt military action.

How can we fight terrorism if governments keep giving in to terrorist demands—as the Japanese government did in Kuala Lumpur when those five Japanese Red Army terrorists took fifty-three hostages?

That's a key problem. There is understandably a good deal of satisfaction that no lives were lost in that incident. But we shouldn't forget that the terrorists got all they demanded—the release of five Red Army terrorist comrades imprisoned in Japan. All ten are now in the Libyan government's hands. We don't know even now, weeks later, what will happen to them, though we greatly hope they will be tried and severely punished. But so far you have another example of a tactically successful terrorist incident.

Each such case is noticed by other potential terrorists around the world.

Wasn't an American diplomat ransomed in that case?

Well, an American consul was one of the hostages, but no ransom was provided by the United States government. In the past, American officials have been ransomed by other governments.

Back in 1969, for example, the Brazilian government released a number of political prisoners so that Ambassador C. Burke Elbrick, taken by terrorists, might be freed.

Has the United States itself ever paid ransom?

No, the United States has never paid ransom—and I hope that is widely known. We have a firm no-ransom policy. We do not pay ransom, release prisoners or otherwise yield to terrorist blackmail. If we met terrorist demands in one place we might save a few lives, but at the risk of hundreds of lives elsewhere.

In the Kuala Lumpur case, the United States stayed completely in the background. There was absolutely no US pressure, no suggestion of any kind how the Malaysian and Japanese governments should handle the matter. That was the concern of the Malaysians, as the host government, and of the Japanese, to whom the terrorists' demands were put.

Types of Terrorism

What is this Japanese Red Army, anyway?

It is a nihilist, world-revolution outfit which had a certain life in Japan before being brought under essential control there by the Japanese authorities. So it turned out into the world to pursue its anti-establishment, revolutionary objectives, tying in with other terrorist groups like the Popular Front for the Liberation of Palestine. The JRA is a tiny group numerically—maybe a score or two of expatriate terrorist types—with negligible support inside Japan.

They're regarded as a disgrace by the great majority of Japanese.

Does the term "Red Army" mean they're Communist?

The JRA has been said to be neither Japanese, nor Red nor an army. There are Communist elements in its theories, but no support from Moscow or Peking that I'm aware of. They want to pull down the existing world structure and start again in some not clearly defined way.

Are there other terrorist groups like this?

The Baader-Meinhof group in West Germany has the same sort of theoretical basis. They, too, are against the establishment. They feel the whole world order stinks and should be redone. Of course, like so many terrorist groups, they're great on destruction but weak on construction.

Are there any Latin-American groups of this nature?

No, the Latin-American terrorist groups have been more domestic-terrorist types with objectives within the country.

Terrorist groups in Argentina, Uruguay and some other countries work together in some degree with exchanges of money, training and so forth. But basically they have their own political objectives inside each country.

Which of these groups seem to be the greatest threat to the United States?

That's hard to say. We've been very lucky in this country that international terrorism really hasn't reached us. We have our domestic-terrorist organizations such as the Weather Underground and a few radical minority groups. And, fortunately, we have a highly effective FBI to deal with threats of this sort.

Palestinian terrorists have not found it profitable to attempt to operate here, except for a few incidents. I imagine the Palestinian terrorist groups would be reluctant, by engaging in terror activities here, to jeopardize the support the Palestinian cause gets in this country.

What real damage has terrorism done to the world?

Well, you have to look at that in two different ways:

In numbers, the terrorist impact has been fairly small. Since 1968, some eight hundred individuals have been killed as a result of international terrorism. About seventeen hundred have been wounded. Year by year, that's no more than the crime rate of one moderate-sized American city.

In political terms, however, terrorism has had a far greater impact than these figures suggest. When you have a situation where air travel can be endangered, where mail must be X-rayed for explosives, where international conferences can be disrupted by bomb threats, where embassies and diplomats can be hampered in their work, where justice is impaired as perpetrators of horrible acts of violence are given short sentences or let free, and where state authority is weakened as governments accede to terrorist demands—then you can see the consequences which uncontrolled terrorism could have. . . .

Just what do you do as Coordinator for Combatting Terrorism?

Well, . . . [in 1972] President Nixon set up a Cabinet Committee to Combat Terrorism. The committee consists of the heads of ten departments and agencies concerned with terrorism, including State, Defense, Justice, the CIA and the FBI. Under the Cabinet committee, which is chaired by [the] Secretary of State . . ., there's a working group on which the above ten and eleven other departments and agencies are represented. I chair that group.

We meet every other week. During terrorist incidents, we set up a task force in the State Department Operations Center to provide centralized direction.

Is there an international organization to fight terrorism?

Not really, no. Other governments have organized themselves, as we have, to deal with their terrorism problems.

The United States has sought mightily to achieve better international cooperation on terrorism through the United Nations and other international bodies, but without great success. A good deal has been accomplished on hijacking

and protection of diplomats, but the conventions have not
been adhered to by a number of key nations, and they lack
enforcement teeth. [For more detailed discussion of US efforts see "American Policy Against Terrorism," by Lewis
Hoffacker, in Section IV, below.]

Fewer Safe Havens

*How many governments, other than Libya, still provide
a haven for terrorists?*

The number has gone steadily down. South Yemen used
to do it. So did Kuwait. No more.

It was really touch and go whether the Malaysian and
Japanese governments could find a place that would accept
the Kuala Lumpur terrorists. Libya did it only at the last
moment.

*Is that the way to end terrorism—get the safe havens
closed down?*

We attach great importance to that. Secretary Kissinger
stressed the point in his August 11 [1975] address in Montreal [at the annual meeting of the American Bar Associa-
tion].

Thus far, however, we have been able to obtain very
little support for conventions which would require governments to prosecute or extradite terrorists coming under
their control in aircraft seeking safe haven or otherwise.

Why?

Many governments are sympathetic with the objectives
of terrorist groups.

Also, governments are often reluctant to crack down on
terrorists because they want to stay on good terms with the
governments that support them. And governments may be
reluctant to seize and jail terrorists because they fear other
terrorists will come to rescue their comrades with new acts
of terrorism.

This adds up to a lot of reluctant governments.

Then how can you fight terrorism?

In a number of ways. One is through intelligence. If you

can learn a terrorist's plans ahead of time you can some-times forestall him. Intelligence led to the discovery of the SA-7 rockets at Rome.

Another area is physical security. We've done a lot in our government, and so have some other governments, to strengthen the security of our airports, diplomatic establish-ments and other target installations and people.

A third is to make terrorism unprofitable for the ter-rorists, mainly by arresting and punishing them.

And a fourth is to eliminate the underlying causes of terrorism—to reduce the inequities and frustrations from which terrorism in varying degree arises. That, clearly, is a long-term proposition.

How about the punishment of terrorists?

The record is poor. An international terrorist involved in a kidnapping has about an 80 percent chance of escaping death or capture. The average sentence for the small pro-portion of terrorists who are caught and tried is only about eighteen months.

How about terrorism for money? What do you tell American businessmen who ask what they should do about terrorist kidnappings for ransom abroad?

Well, we start by urging them to do everything possible to protect themselves against kidnapping. We also tell them that, if it happens, we think they should follow our gov-ernment's no-ransom policy.

If not resisted, kidnapping feeds on its successes. But we have no legal means to restrain a company that decides to meet a ransom demand. In Argentina, particularly, Ameri-can and other companies have paid big ransoms. And kid-nappings and the size of demands there have steadily in-creased.

Would you say that international terrorism would pros-per in the United States?

No. The FBI's record in ordinary criminal kidnappings and in dealing with domestic-terrorist organizations is not one to encourage international terrorists.

The recent kidnapping of the Philippine ambassador in Washington was handled most effectively by the FBI, the Washington Metropolitan Police and other agencies. The ambassador was released unharmed and the terrorist caught, tried and convicted.

Fish must swim in the sea, and there is little sea, in the sense of public approval or tolerance of terrorists here. But we must be on our guard, as we are. Our government is seeking with all the energy and imagination it can muster to deal with the international-terrorist threat abroad and to prevent it from developing here.

II. VARIETIES OF MODERN TERRORISM

EDITOR'S INTRODUCTION

Curiously, although open, democratic societies seem most vulnerable to terrorist threats, the actual origin of modern terrorism in its most popular form of airplane hijacking can be traced to Eastern Europe in the years immediately following World War II. It was there that desperate men and women fleeing for their lives took to commandeering commercial airliners and diverting them, at gunpoint, to safe havens. When the practice spread to US hijackers bent on flying to Cuba, liberal democracies grew alarmed.

The motivations of modern terrorism range from simple greed through a broad spectrum of political causes and grievances that often enough the terrorist himself fails to understand rationally. One distinguishing feature of modern terrorism is that the human being holding the gun or bomb appears less concerned with the triumph of his cause than with the expression of it. Most terrorists have only the vaguest idea of what must be done to eliminate their grievances. This is not to say that terrorism is wholly irrational—a private pastime of psychotics. The sampling of terrorist causes around the world included in this chapter attests to the variety of well-known causes espoused.

The first article, taken from the *New Republic,* surveys the broad range of political malcontents at work throughout Europe. In the following article William Mathewson of the *Wall Street Journal* details an episode involving one of these groups in Holland and notes in particular the lingering anguish of the chance victims of the terrorists' demands. Then an article, from the New York *Times,* notes the particular vulnerability of West Germany to recent terrorist assault.

The next article, from *Current History*, surveys the continuing activities of Arab terrorists in the Middle East and the potential there for escalation to nuclear terror. Recent press reports revealing that a student at Princeton University had written a thesis on the making of an atomic bomb for a few thousand dollars make this article especially frightening.

In the fifth article, Robert A. Fearey, formerly US Coordinator for Combatting Terrorism, presents a full exposition of the nature, causes, and extent of international terrorism in our time. Despite certain tactical successes, he notes, terrorist groups have yet to attain their fundamental political goals.

The section concludes with an article that focuses on terrorist activities in the United States.

EUROPE UNDER THE GUN [1]

For a generation there was a general assumption that post-industrial Europe was immune to the more violent fashions in political extremism. One Budapest appeared enough to demonstrate the stability of the authoritarian East, and one Paris spring to show the irrelevance of the barricades in the West. If there were to be illicit change, it would come in the more traditional form of a formal and bloodless military coup, as has been the case in Greece and Portugal—and even then democracy appeared the ultimate winner. If terrorists did appear in Europe at Rome airport or the Olympics, they were driven by distant motives, bringing with them the violence of the periphery. If Algerians were fished from the Seine, they were, after all, Algerians. Thus when Northern Ireland slowly collapsed into chaos after 1970, the violence seemed incomprehensible to most

[1] From "The Gun in Europe," by J. Bowyer Bell, academic expert on terrorism, author of *The Myth of the Guerrilla*, *On Revolt*, and *Terror Out of Zion*. *New Republic*. 173:10-12. N. 22, '75. Reprinted by permission. Dr. Bell has taught at Harvard and MIT and is presently associated with the Institute of War and Peace Studies at Columbia University.

observers, the child of Celtic malice, a religious war in the twentieth century. The fact is that in recent years Europe has become a battlefield for all sorts and conditions of secret armies engaged in liberating unsuspected or unwilling nations from previously unnoticed oppressors. Much of Western Europe has become a free fire zone for this new and violent generation of guerrillas.

In . . . [1975], two Turkish ambassadors have been assassinated in Vienna and Paris, a Dutch businessman kidnapped in Ireland, Spanish police shot down in the streets of Madrid, a car bombed in London, another kidnapping in Italy, more bombs in Portugal and a massive, worldwide display of indignation at the execution of Spanish revolutionaries. A quick flutter through last year's newspapers reveals that this is by no means a special or particularly violent period. Even to the optimistic there appears to be more trouble in store for Portugal, for Spain, even for Italy, and there are always the Irish. The pessimists foresee an era of revolt and reaction that may seriously strain European stability. In a large degree it has been that very stability, the economic miracle, the free movement of working populations, the easing of old tensions, the consumer revolution—all the supposedly good things of the new European life that have been responsible for the rising resort to violence by the few. Many nationalists see this next generation as crucial; independence must be achieved before all Europe slips into a homogenized Coke-culture. Now is the time for a united Ireland, a Welsh republic, a free Brittany or Corsica or Catalonia before the language is lost, before the iron laws of the Common Market drain off the people to the Saar and replace them with German tourists, before the European edges become parklands. Then there are those on the Left who see an apparently indestructible post-imperial system of oppression, a system that buys the workers' loyalty with color television sets—the opiate of the people—a system so complacent, so coercive, that only terror can engender change. And finally on the Right are men who abhor the drift to secularism or to the acceptance of the Communists as respectable or to Americanization. They speak for the old values, the old ways. They speak with the bomb.

Encouraging Extremism

Europe is currently most vulnerable to the bomber. An Italian anarchist can drift through the restaurant underground of London without attracting notice. Greeks in Volkswagens are everywhere to be found. The Irish are in Liverpool, the Basques in Paris, and the components of infernal devices easy to purchase. And there are so many soft and symbolic targets: the giant national airlines, the embassies, the computers and prime ministers and refineries. When driven and dedicated men are determined to act no matter what the risk, the forces of order are sorely pressed. In Germany the spectacular operations choreographed by the Baader-Meinhof group forced the security forces into an intense, extremely expensive anti-terrorist campaign. Even the present trial of some of the members is being held in a huge, high security structure built solely for the event. A very few can produce the most disproportionate results; a single dramatic operation can be magnified by television; one person can change history.

What is crucially important is that Europe can rumble along under such a threat. The various bombing campaigns of World War II by the Allies and the Axis dumped far more tonnage on the vulnerable than any terrorist is likely to do; but mostly life then was more uncomfortable, more dangerous, and until near the end everyone coped. Despite all their bombs the Provisional IRA [Irish Republican Army] has not been able to force the British to evacuate Northern Ireland—yet. No one can really take seriously a grasp for power by the Red Brigades in Italy or the new breed of German revolutionary. What is far more likely and far from a pleasing prospect is that the gunmen may unwittingly either unleash the forces of reaction or precipitate a civil war. And some of the more radically inclined revolutionaries feel that either eventuality will ultimately reward them.

In the past few years in Italy there has been a revival of revolutionary fascism. As early as 1948 a Black Legion of the unrepentant was formed in Northern Italy. Broken up by the authorities in 1951, it reappeared in 1954 as the New Order. In April 1974, the name changed to the Political Movement of New Order and from that to the Black Order. All this elaborate verbiage may cover as few as three hundred militants but there are similar militant groups, mostly north of Rome, some linked by loose ties but all dedicated to violence. This new Fascist underground in Italy assumes that if they can create a rising level of chaos at the same time the Italian Communist party creeps closer to power there will be another march on Rome.

There are those in Ireland who can envisage that a doomsday situation in the north—civil war without a British referee—will create a situation in Dublin to the advantage of *real* Irish republicans.

The Provisional IRA that arose out of the sectarian troubles of 1969–1971 has waged, until the recent truce, a classic insurgent campaign against the British army. With several thousand members, especially effective in the Catholic ghettos of Belfast and Derry and certain rural areas, with arms and money seeping in from abroad, with friends to the south in the Irish republic, the Provos under the hardliner Seamus Twomey all but hold a veto in regard to British policy options in Ulster. Their Republican rivals, the Official IRA, somewhat smaller, more radical under Cathal Goulding and Sean Goulding, is no whit less violent and perhaps more talented. The latest Republican splinter, the couple of hundred Irish Republican Socialist party of Seamus Costello, broke away from the Officials as too tame. All of these groups plus independents and individuals, the hard men of Irish politics, agree at least on one principle: Ireland was divided by force and will be united by force,

and some are not beyond detonating bombs in Birmingham
to underline their logic.

Not all the revolutionaries have such luminous dreams
of a terrible beauty born out of a blood bath, but then a few
shots in the right place might just do the trick.

And there are throughout Europe these small groups—a
hundred ill-organized Corsicans or a dozen Cypriot Greeks
—quite willing to shoot. Some, in fact, have been shooting
for years without, until recently, attracting any great interest. The Basque liberation front of ETA, split not unlike
the IRA into a political and militant wing, has for a decade
been involved in a separatist campaign. They have a few
hundred activists, often in exile, but tens of thousands of
sympathizers. At times Spanish repression has reduced the
militants to a handful, pursued even into their French
sanctuaries by police gunmen. But they have persisted . . .
assassinating Prime Minister Admiral Luis Carrero Blanco
in the process. Now under extreme pressure after the executions and waves of arrests, ETA gunmen can shoot down
police on the streets of Madrid.

Spotlight on Spain

There is at the moment no place so vulnerable to the
inappropriate shot as Spain. A long forty years have passed
since the civil war. The immunization has been wearing off,
for a new generation appears willing to take risks without
their fathers' experience of the costs involved even if by
miscalculation. No matter that all the more formal underground parties insist they want nothing more than democracy, toleration, civil liberties and a peaceful transition to
the post–Franco era. There are those, well-armed and in
power, who believe that democracy is a code word for deca-
dence, that civil liberties open the door to paganism, and
that toleration would destroy the state. How, indeed, can
Spain tolerate a Basque republic? And for the Basque guerrillas why should they assume any Spanish government
would acquiesce in secession, or any French government?

Even a wise and talented government in Madrid would have great difficulty in creating a federal Spain. And it has been a very long time since a wise and talented government met in Madrid. The pent-up frustrations of four decades, the nationality problem aside, will be difficult to control, the demand for vengeance real, the fears of the powerful and contented extreme. With gunmen on the street the prospects for an era of good feeling appear bleak. Only oppression has been able to maintain order in modern Spain and a continuation of the old system no longer seems a possible option; a police state can run short of policemen. Moderation, compromise and accommodation may indeed be about to have their day. The sensible will recognize the risks, ignore the bombers and the old quarrels and move on. Yet restraint and sweet reason have always had few takers in Spain.

If elsewhere in Europe the prospects do not seem quite so bleak, only in Scandinavia does there appear real stability. The Irish troubles go on and on; no one can see how things can get better and everyone knows they could get worse. There have been bombs in Scotland and Wales. The Bretons and Corsicans could, again, choose violence. All the Italian political parties are concerned with the men at the fringe. There are Croatian guerrillas, German anarchists, Portuguese Maoists, all waiting in the wings. There are language problems in Belgium and Switzerland, cultural separatists in France, irredentists in northern Italy, and always the transients: Palestinian fedayeen [guerrillas against Israel], EOKA-B Cypriots [Greek underground organization], the Japanese Red Army. [For further information on the Red Army, see "Sizing Up the Menace," in Section I, above and "The Ever-Violent Middle East," by L. R. Beres, in this section, below.—Ed.] And Europe makes a splendid stage to play out their ambitions with violent deeds. One hopes those in power recognize that the revolutionary threat is not lethal but tolerable. Few want a march on Rome or a Spanish Civil War but without care neither is impossible. The gunman knows that, and so he has written in a role for his opponent.

Too often the role seems likely to be attractive to the threatened. Car bombs and dead policemen produce indignation and a demand for action, an end to terrorism. Outraged indignation should fit uncomfortably on those who gave us the holocaust or the fire bombing of Hamburg or a century of large scale brutality, but it does not. More to the point, such indignation is partisan. The wave of protest over the Spanish executions indicates that some gunmen are more acceptable than others, especially if they have an odious enemy in a distant country. Thus some may approve of the Red brigades but not the Black; Irish unity but not Spanish; cultural independence, but only for foreigners. One man's terrorist is another's patriot. From the seat of power in Rome or London or Madrid the gunmen are wicked, evil men who must be destroyed by any means, by all means. And therein lies the danger. Without a sense of proportion, the effort to get terror by the throat, end murder from the ditch, may do more damage to order than to the gunmen.

INCIDENT IN HOLLAND [2]

On the Dutch calendar of holidays, December 5 is set aside in honor of St. Nicholas and is a day when presents are exchanged. Therefore, on the morning of December 2, 1975, three days before St. Nicholas Day, the appearance of seven youths bearing brightly wrapped gifts wasn't a sight that aroused much attention on the train-station platform in this northern Dutch town [Assen].

But to one of the bystanders, all of whom were waiting for the 9:53 A.M. train to Amsterdam, there *was* something faintly incongruous about the young men and their parcels.

[2] From "Bitterness Surrounding Dutch Train Hijacking Lingers a Year Later," by William Mathewson, staff reporter. *Wall Street Journal.* 189:1+. Ja. 6, '77. Reprinted with permission of the *Wall Street Journal* © 1977 Dow Jones & Company Inc. All Rights Reserved.

"The packages were of abnormal size—very large. That caught my attention first," recalls Hans Prins, a radiobiologist who was heading for Hoogeveen, a twenty-minute train trip, to deliver some blood samples to a laboratory. "Then I noticed that the men were Moluccans, or at least I thought they were Moluccans."

Mr. Prins's immediate reaction was alarm. It was a biased reaction, he admits, but it wasn't without some justification. Descendants of the South Moluccans who had been expatriated to Holland from what now is part of Indonesia in the years following the Second World War had been agitating for years to return to an independent island republic. In 1970, a group of South Moluccans had stormed the Indonesian Embassy in The Hague, killing a Dutch policeman before being captured. Then in April 1975, several South Moluccans were arrested following discovery of a plot to kidnap Queen Juliana.

In any case, Mr. Prins's first thought was to report the youths to the stationmaster, for he feared that they might be carrying weapons in the parcels. But the train was due in a matter of minutes, and fear of embarrassment quickly overcame his alarm. If the youths *weren't* armed, he thought, he would feel like a fool if they were stopped and searched on his suspicions. And yet . . .

Before he could make up his mind, the train pulled into the station. It was a train typical of those used on many domestic runs in Holland: Two spacious cars, with the driver's cab in the front of the first car. It isn't known exactly how many passengers were aboard when the train arrived in Assen shortly before 10 A.M., nor how many passengers got on or off at Assen or at Beilen, the next stop some ten minutes away. But when the train left the Beilen station it is believed that there were eighty-odd persons aboard.

It normally takes a train about nine minutes to go from Beilen to Hoogeveen, the next stop. But just south of Beilen on this morning, the train stopped. "Moluccans seemed to come pouring into the compartment," Mr. Prins recalls.

(The South Moluccan youths had been in an antechamber outside the main compartment of the first car; they had pulled an emergency brake to stop the train.) "They had sten guns, rifles and revolvers. They said, 'This is a hijacking. Anybody who moves is dead.' "

Thus began what came to be called the Dutch Train Incident, yet another entry in the ever-growing chronicle of acts of political terrorism around the world. Before its climax after twelve harrowing days and nights, three hostages would die, the routine of the Dutch government would be virtually paralyzed and part of the attention of much of the world would be focused on the dispatches and broadcasts of the three hundred reporters on the scene.

Today, more than a year later, the "incident" is largely forgotten outside Holland. But for many of those involved it was an ordeal that still goes on. The hijackers—all of whom were captured, tried and convicted—are serving fourteen-year prison terms. For some of the passengers there are continuing fears, recurring nightmares and new phobias. Less expected are the harsh criticisms by some of the passengers, not toward the hijackers, but toward the government. It is an atmosphere of lingering bitterness that has been aggravated by the shift of world attention to other, fresher terrorist crimes.

Gaining Publicity

For the South Moluccan expatriates themselves, in whose name the crime was committed, it is generally conceded that the hijacking brought some gains—even if the immediate gains were no more than publicity for a group virtually unknown outside the Netherlands and the Far East.

"Who the hell are the South Moluccans?" asked one newspaper reporter arriving on the scene of the hijacking. It isn't a question that has a simple answer, but an answer is necessary before exploring the details of the hijacking, its conception and its aftermath.

The seeds of many of today's terrorist acts were sown

long ago, germinated by wars and political upheavals, nurtured over the years by resentment and brought into full flower by any of a host of random events. Such was the case with the hijack of the Dutch train, which had its beginnings in the South Molucca Islands, one hundred miles west of New Guinea. Once known as the Spice Islands and long under the control of the Dutch colonial empire, the South Moluccas were given up by the Netherlands in 1949.

The plan was absorption into Indonesia. However, a faction of Moluccans, many of whom had fought on the side of the Dutch during World War II, wanted independence and revolted against their new rulers in Jakarta. The revolt (the first of several) was crushed, and in 1950, some 12,000 South Moluccans chose to emigrate to Holland. At that time, the Dutch talked of one day returning the group to an independent republic.

It was a goal without much substance. But it wasn't seen as such by many of the expatriate Moluccans or, more particularly, by their children. For while the first-generation Moluccan immigrants here had lived by a tradition of patient service to the Dutch, the second generation had begun to look upon their parents as, at best, obsequious and, at worst, traitors to the cause of independence.

By the mid-1970s, the population of South Moluccans in the Netherlands had grown to between 30,000 and 40,000.

They are mostly people without an identity [says Dick Mulder, a psychiatrist who works with the Netherlands Department of Justice]. Their language came from Indonesia, their religion from the Dutch. They don't have their own culture or their own fatherland. The second generation feels deprived. It wants to be something. It wants a new identity.

Against this background, two events occurred in 1975 that were to have far-reaching implications for the Moluccans and their cause. The first was the arrest of four Palestinians in Amsterdam for plotting the hijack of a train carrying Russian Jews from Warsaw to various points in Holland. The plot was unsuccessful, but the attendant publicity gave a few young South Moluccans something to think about, as one of the Dutch train's hijackers later admitted in court.

Then, on November 25, Queen Juliana delivered a speech on the occasion of the independence of Surinam, a former Dutch colony. "All peoples have a right to their own country," she said. This was later said to be the spark that ignited the hijacking plot.

The plot was very much an amateur's affair; the seven young men weren't trained by outside forces, nor was there any elaborate financing required. (It hasn't been determined where they obtained their weapons, but it is said to be relatively easy to obtain firearms in Holland.)

Certainly, it wasn't a plot that depended on split-second timing; almost any train would serve their purpose. On the morning of December 2, the hijackers, all of whom were in their twenties and residents of Bovens-Milde, near Assen, boarded a public bus for the short trip to the Assen train station.

It was crucial that the hijackers quickly take control of whatever train they selected. This they did in the first seconds after they brought the Amsterdam-bound train to a halt. Indeed, their control was horrifyingly obvious to everyone aboard when they almost immediately shot the train's driver to death for resisting the takeover.

The terrorists' next step was to release three passengers— two women and a child—with instructions to carry a written set of demands to the next crossing. The Moluccans' chief demands were for a bus to carry them and their hostages to Amsterdam's Schiphol Airport and for a plane to fly the group to an unstated destination. The hijackers asserted that if the bus didn't arrive by 1 P.M., some two hours away, a passenger would be killed.

A Plea for Mercy

That deadline came and went, and no bus arrived. At 1:30, one of the hijackers, twenty-five-year-old Paul Saimima, selected a passenger to be executed: thirty-three-year-old Rob de Groot, a real-estate dealer. Mr. de Groot was marched to an open train door. Saimima instructed an accomplice, twenty-three-year-old Eliza Hahury to shoot. Mr. de Groot, pleading for his life, said he wanted to pray. Hahury fired, but the shot missed and the hostage ran to freedom.

The next person singled out wasn't so fortunate. At about two o'clock, Saimima selected Leo Bulters, a twenty-year-old soldier. As with Mr. de Groot, the young conscript was taken to the train door. Hahury fired the first shot, and the victim, his hands tied behind his back, fell from the train. He wasn't yet dead, and so Saimima and a third terrorist finished the execution with more shots.

During those first hours, the train was surrounded by police marksmen and army troops. However, it wasn't until after nightfall that the Dutch government made a formal response to the hijackers' demand for safe conduct out of the country. "We have never given in to such demands . . . and we shall not give in now," said Andreas van Agt, Minister of Justice.

By the end of the first day, it became clear that the hijackers didn't have complete control of the train. The terrorists were all in the first car, which couldn't be reached from the second car. This left the second car effectively unguarded. Although the hijackers had warned passengers in the second car that they would be shot if they tried to escape, half of the twenty-seven rear-car passengers sneaked off the train without incident before dawn of the hijacking's second day.

By then, the Dutch government had set up a so-called crisis center in Beilen. A field telephone was installed linking the train with a farm a few hundred feet away. At the farm, a few policemen and a "spokesman" were hooked up to the crisis center, which was manned by local and provincial authorities, a psychiatrist and a psychologist. The crisis center in turn reported to the central government in The Hague.

From The Hague that day came another message from

Mr. van Agt, the Minister of Justice: Force might be used against the terrorists if the hijacking continued much longer.

The hijackers made another demand for a bus to be delivered, this time with a deadline of 10 A.M. the following day. If the deadline wasn't met, the hijackers said, another passenger would be killed.

As the deadline passed, authorities stuck to their position that the hijackers wouldn't be moved. The hijackers' first response was to extend the deadline by a few hours; however they soon decided that it would be necessary to kill another passenger.

But before they could act, the situation was abruptly transformed. Shortly after noon, another group of young South Moluccans, also seven in number, invaded the Indonesian consulate in Amsterdam, seizing more than thirty-two hostages, including seventeen children attending school there.

No sooner was attention focused on Amsterdam, than it reverted back to Beilen as, in the middle of the afternoon, another body fell from the train. The victim was a thirty-two-year-old man. The hijackers shot him in the head as he knelt, hands tied behind his back in the doorway.

It still isn't clear whether the invasion of the consulate had been coordinated with the train hijacking. But according to government authorities, the two terrorist factions came from the same group, grew up together and had the same way of presenting their demands.

Three Principal Demands

The principal demands of both groups were three: The release of all South Moluccan political prisoners in Indonesia; the freedom of South Moluccans in their homeland to discuss forming a republic; and a meeting between Indonesia's President Suharto and Jan Manusama, the president of the so-called South Moluccan government in exile.

Indonesia rejected the demands out of hand. And on

Friday, December 5, the day following the consulate invasion and the fourth day of the train hijacking, the Dutch Prime Minister, Joop den Uyl, reaffirmed that none of the terrorists would be allowed to leave Holland.

Leaders of the South Moluccan community tried to reason with the terrorists from the very beginning. Mr. Manusama spent three hours on December 11 on the train; the result was the release of two elderly hostages. The Rev. Samuel Metiari, a Moluccan clergyman, was able to effect the release of some of the children at the consulate. But the role of these mediators is still being debated. Some hostages credit them with ending the incident, others think they had little effect.

The Justice Department's Dr. Mulder, who was in communication with the terrorists at both the Indonesian consulate and a Dutch prison siege in 1974, sees a similarity among many hostage cases and says authorities can benefit by knowing about this similarity. Almost always, he says, such cases can be divided into three separate phases. The train incident was no exception.

The first phase is a period of chaos and uncertainty and the reversal of traditional power roles. "Suddenly [the hijackers] have the power that they have lacked for years," he says. "Just as suddenly, the victims have no power at all. They can't even urinate without permission. It is somewhat the same helpless feeling as that of the hospital patient."

According to Dr. Mulder, psychiatrists have learned that it is important during this phase to freeze the situation. "The terrorists must be treated as if they have power—because they *do* have power. . . . If they ask for food, give it to them, but say you will give it to them at nine o'clock, again at noon and then at six. In other words, structure them in a dependent way."

In phase two, he says, "a sense of reality returns." A dialogue of sorts begins between the terrorists and their hostages, who begin to learn more about one another.

In the third and final phase, he says, "the terrorists want

to give up but they can't initially allow themselves to give in to these feelings because it would mean that they have failed."

During this period, Dr. Mulder says, it is important for the authorities to gain the hijackers' trust. "One must speak of 'we,' rather than 'you' and 'me' when speaking to the hijackers," he says. "The idea is that 'we' are all in the same boat and it is going the wrong way. Only 'we' can turn it around together."

During this phase, a sympathetic link develops between hijackers and their prisoners. "At first the victims think the terrorists are terrible," Dr. Mulder says. Then through prolonged contact, with the terrorists explaining what drove them to their act, the victim begins to see that their cause may be a just one.

At the same time, Dr. Mulder says, the captives begin to internalize their anger and aggression toward the hijackers. Because aggression can't be internalized forever, it is rechanneled elsewhere, and the most convenient target is often the authorities.

At Last Surrender

As passengers and authorities recall, the three phases occurred more or less as predicted on the train until December 14, when the hijackers surrendered. The consulate was in captivity until December 19. The toll on the train was three dead hostages and one wounded terrorist. (He was injured when a gun went off by accident.) At the consulate, the only fatality was one hostage, who died after he jumped from a window on the first day of the captivity.

The consulate hostages haven't been critical of the government (not surprising, considering that most of them were diplomats in a foreign country). But for many of the former captives on the train, phase three seems to go on.

"We all feel betrayed," says Hans Prins, who has emerged as a sort of unofficial spokesman for the train hostages. In essence, Mr. Prins explains, the hostages feel that the government ignored them once the hijacking was over. For example, he says, one of the hostages refused last summer to pay a traffic ticket because he hadn't been reimbursed by the government for a coat that had been used by the hijackers to cover the corpse of one of their victims. Some of the hostages have met with government officials, Mr. Prins says, but with few results. "We haven't even been asked if there are any financial damages," he says.

The government admits that it had made errors. For example, during the captivity, spokesmen assured reporters that the train passengers weren't undergoing any undue discomforts. This was done to calm relatives, a government official says; but authorities now think it was an unwise move, because hostages later claimed that the government had blithely minimized their ordeal.

Hostages also claim that the government didn't respond quickly enough to the hijackers' demands, thereby endangering lives. One government official concedes that the communications process was cumbersome.

But the biggest mistake—and this is conceded by several officials—was assuming that the hostages would simply want to resume their pre-siege lives and forget what happened to them.

Here were these people elevated from obscurity to the limelight [says one government official]. Then all of a sudden the limelight is extinguished. Everything is over. What should have been done was to let the limelight dim gradually. Give them medals. Give them recognition. We were too busy for that and it was wrong.

According to Dr. Mulder, it would have been fruitful if the government had approached the newly released hostages and asked them to detail what happened to them. "Say to the hostages, 'We need your help. Give us your experiences.'" Not only would this be genuinely useful during future sieges but, he says, it would help to undermine the hostages' aggression.

A year after the hijacking, the government and the hostages are farther apart than ever, with the hostages talking of suing the government for an alleged coverup of its inadequacies during the siege. On the plus side, the government has created a commission to look into bettering relations with the immigrant South Moluccan population.

Also on the plus side, at least as far as the government is concerned, are the lessons learned last year. It has instituted a series of lectures to policemen, public prosecutors and local officials throughout the country. "You can't ever completely prepare everybody" for a siege, a Justice Department official says. "But the more everybody knows, the better it is."

[On May 23, 1977, South Moluccan exiles living in the Netherlands were holding 161 hostages in an elementary school and a hijacked train, in a new effort to force the Dutch government to help them in their fight for independence of their homeland from Indonesia. The school children were released May 26 when they became ill. Subsequently, 3 of the captives on the train and one of the teachers in the school were also released, one at a time, because they urgently needed medical attention. Then, after nearly three weeks of negotiations, the government decided to take action. On June 11 a platoon of 30 marines attacked the train and another group freed the teachers held in the school. Two of the train passengers and six of the South Moluccans were killed in the action.—Ed.]

GERMANY IN THRALL [3]

The French decision to free Abu Daoud [Palestinian leader alleged to have planned the Munich massacre of Israeli athletes in 1972] set off a wave of righteous indignation in West Germany, which was getting ready, a little too ponderously, to request his extradition on murder charges connected with the massacre at the Munich Olympic Games in 1972. But there were some officials here who were relieved they didn't get him.

[3] From "Bonn Wasn't Eager to Extradite Abu Daoud," by Craig R. Whitney, Bonn correspondent. New York *Times*. p E2. Ja. 23, '77. © 1977 by The New York Times Company. Reprinted by permission.

The Germans weren't being hypocritical, according to people with serious interest in the case—Israeli and United States diplomats, for instance—even though their delay in formally requesting extradition was one reason the French court used for freeing the accused terrorist.

Abu Daoud had a dangerous connection to the German "Baader-Meinhof gang," a violent, pseudo-revolutionary group that has caused serious distortions in the fabric of democracy [in Germany] and has a potential for more damage.

With Mr. Daoud in a West German jail, there could have been reprisals from other Palestinians and from German radical terrorists still at large, another nightmare of bombings, deaths, and restrictions on civil liberties.

Even though most of the "Baader-Meinhof" radicals are now behind bars, terrorism is still a real danger in Europe, and increasingly an international one. This became dramatically clear . . . [in July 1976] when members of the Popular Front for the Liberation of Palestine hijacked an Air France jet and its Israeli passengers to Entebbe, Uganda. There were two Germans among the terrorists, probably Wilfried Bose and Brigitte Kuhlmann, both former university students who had disappeared into the Frankfurt underground of communes, "revolutionary cells" and left-wing lawyers. Mr. Bose and Miss Kuhlmann were killed by the Israeli raiders who freed the 103 hostages.

But when "Operation Entebbe," a film about the affair, opened in West Germany early this month, student radicals protested in West Berlin and two theaters elsewhere were bombed.

Strain on German Social Fabric

Terrorist violence has put the West German government and the social order under severe strain. To many critics, what a few fanatic apostles of violence caused this society to do to itself was more worrisome than the actual bombings and murders. Lawyer-client privileges have been violatd, confidence in the impartiality of West German justice shaken and a climate of growing intolerance has replaced the liberality of the early Willy Brandt years.

In their own defense, the Germans say that the "Red Army faction," as Ulrike Meinhof and Andreas Baader called their group, were not just harmless romantics.

Miss Meinhof, who hanged herself in the heavily guarded prison-courtroom complex outside Stuttgart last May [1976], was an orphan who was raised by Roman Catholic nuns and who was married to a left-wing journalist. Mr. Baader, who is now in the twelfth month of his trial in Stuttgart, grew up without a father, did poorly in school, and developed a malignant fascination with explosives. Holger Meins, the fifth original defendant in the trial, died after a hunger strike in November 1974. Gudrun Ensslin and Karl Raspe, the other two surviving members, are former students.

They hoped to start an armed revolution of the "oppressed" German working class. When the masses ignored them, as did the middle class, they declared their own war on United States imperialism, German capitalism, and the institutions of the state. After a series of bank robberies in Berlin in 1970, Mr. Baader and Miss Meinhof went underground and, almost immediately, to the Middle East. In Jordan, they trained in the tactics of guerrilla warfare with the radical Palestinians.

That was the year King Hussein drove the Palestinian guerrillas from Jordan, and the radical Palestinian movement, Black September, was born. Being there may have confirmed the German group in their fanaticism, and it apparently cemented their alliance with the radical Arab movements. They returned home but after a series of bombings that killed four United States soldiers in Heidelberg and Frankfurt in 1972, they were caught by the police.

Despite their arrests, the violence continued. In February 1975, the Second of June Movement, a splinter group related to the Baader-Meinhof faction, kidnapped the Christian Democratic mayoral candidate in West Berlin just before the elections and demanded the release of five of their jailed comrades. Chancellor Helmut Schmidt's government capitulated and flew the prisoners to Aden, in South Yemen. Just before Christmas of 1975, a group under the leadership of the much-wanted international terrorist leader known as "Carlos" [Ilitch Ramirez Sanchez, Venezuelan terrorist] kidnapped eleven Arab and South American oil ministers in Vienna. At least two Germans were believed to have participated.

By that time, Mr. Schmidt had decided capitulation to terrorists was a mistake. When six German guerrillas stormed Bonn's Embassy in Stockholm in April 1975 to try to extort the release of twenty-six Baader-Meinhof defendants, the government stood firm. Three people died in the explosion and shootout that followed, but the surviving terrorists were captured.

The official toughness was the best reason to believe Bonn's assurances of good faith in the Abu Daoud affair. ... [In 1976] after one of the terrorists who had been flown to Aden, Rolf Pohle, was captured by the Athens police, the West Germans asked for his extradition and got it after a fight in the Greek courts. But the fact that there are about 110 terrorists in German jails also makes officials nervous about reprisals by the others still at large—50 to 60 of them, according to the Justice ministry.

Tough Anti-Terrorist Laws

Bonn's perception of the danger has led it to what has been criticized as overreaction. This, and not revolution, may be the most lasting change the Baader-Meinhof group brought to German society. Since last September [1976], "terrorist conspiracy" has been a federal crime, carrying heavy penalties. The authorities can now keep such defendants in jail for as long as five years before trial, with no recourse to habeas corpus. Mail between suspected terrorists under arrest and their lawyers can also be opened and read by the courts. Thanks to a special law designed to cope with the terrorists' contempt for "show trials," the proceedings in Stuttgart have been conducted largely without the defendants.

[In 1976] parliament made it illegal to publish "unconstitutional support of violent acts, or incitement to violence." It sounds well-intentioned, but could a German writer reprint Karl Marx's 1848 Manifesto in 1977? Heinrich Böll, a courageous opponent of anti-terrorist excesses in Germany, wonders.

Otto Schily, a lawyer in the Stuttgart case, said: "My clients were going to be found guilty the day the trial began, on May 21, 1975." He fully expects a penalty of life imprisonment for Mr. Baader, Miss Ensslin and Mr. Raspe.... [In January 1977] he appealed for a mistrial because one of the judges in the Stuttgart Appeals Court had leaked information on the case to the conservative newspaper *Die Welt*, after obtaining documents from his good friend, Judge Theodor Prinzing, who had been presiding over the long trial since the beginning. . . . In a major surprise, Judge Prinzing was removed from the case for "apparent partiality." But the trial . . . resume[d] . . . under his deputy.

THE EVER-VIOLENT MIDDLE EAST [4]

Only a few years ago, accounts of mankind's high-velocity drift toward a nuclear Armaggedon were confined to the risk of war between the United States and the Soviet Union. Today, however, such accounts are essentially different. With more than fifty major terrorist groups operating in the world, many in the Middle East, terrorist activity may well lead to nuclear destruction.

Who are the terrorists in the Middle East? The configuration of bonds and breaks among terrorist groups in the Middle East is sometimes difficult to untangle, nonetheless, the latest available information suggests the following: The

[4] From "Terrorism and the Nuclear Threat in the Middle East," by Louis René Beres, associate professor of political science, Purdue University. *Current History*. 70:27-9. Ja. '76. Reprinted by permission of Current History, Inc.

Palestine Liberation Organization led by Yasir Arafat represents the umbrella group of the Palestinian terrorist movement. The constituent groups of the PLO are represented on the Palestine National Council, with 165 members. Power becomes more concentrated at the level of the fourteen-member Central Committee and the twelve-member Executive Committee chaired by Arafat.

Within these bodies, Al Fatah is the biggest and probably most powerful terrorist group. Black September, a name which symbolizes the wrath of Palestinian terrorists at their suppression by Jordanian King Hussein in September 1970, is essentially a "spin off" of Al Fatah. After Al Fatah, the most important terrorist group is the Popular Front for the Liberation of Palestine (PFLP). The PFLP made its appearance in November 1967 (Al Fatah came into existence as a secret movement for the liberation of Palestine some eleven years earlier), merging two smaller groups, the Heroes of the Return and the Palestinian faction of the Movement of Arab Nationalists.

Since then, at least three splinter groups have left the Marxist-Leninist PFLP: the Popular Democratic Front for the Liberation of Palestine; the Za'rur group; and the Jibril group. Today, George Habash, chief of the PFLP, appears to be in serious conflict with Arafat. Consequently, three main groups of the PLO—Al Fatah, the Syrian-backed Al Saiqa, and Naif Hawatmeh's Popular Democratic Front —are under continuing pressure to adopt a more extreme line, defined by dissident Palestinian factions of the so-called Rejection Front led by Habash.

The Nuclear Danger

Nuclear weapons may well be used by these terrorist groups, partly because of the increased availability of nuclear weapons, either by theft of assembled systems from military stockpiles or by self-development from weapon-grade plutonium pilfered from nuclear power plants. In the case of theft of an assembled weapon, determined terrorist operatives might direct their attention to any of the thousands of tactical nuclear weapons now deployed across the world by the United States, its allies, and the Soviet Union.

How difficult would it be to carry out such a feat? According to the highly regarded *Defense Monitor*, a publication of the Center for Defense Information in Washington, D.C.:

U.S. Army Special Forces exercises have shown that nuclear weapons storage areas can be penetrated successfully wthout detection despite guards, fences, and sensors. Their example could obviously be followed by a daring and well-organized terrorist organization.

As the available supply of fossil fuels continues to be depleted, states will turn to nuclear power for energy needs. Unfortunately, the by-products of fission in the nuclear plant are the basic material for a fission bomb or radiation dispersal device. Hence, as increasingly large amounts of plutonium-239 are produced by the nuclear power industry in the years ahead, there will be growing opportunity for terrorists to exploit the possibilities of nuclear fuel.

How difficult would it be for terrorists to secure substantial amounts of plutonium? According to Mason Willrich and Theodore Taylor the safeguards are so inadequate that it is only a matter of time before terrorists are able to remove essential fissionable materials from nuclear power plants surreptitiously [*Nuclear Theft: Risks and Safeguards,* Ballinger, 1974]. Indeed, even if appropriate steps to improve nuclear safeguards are taken in this country, genuine protection of fissionable materials from terrorist groups must be global in scope. (Steps to correct some of the most atrocious deficiencies in the American safeguards system—e.g., storage of large amounts of plutonium in buildings secured only by conventional locks, cross-country shipment of plutonium in unguarded trucks—were taken pursuant to a report by the General Accounting Office to the Congress in November 1973.)

According to nuclear physicist Ralph Lapp, a dedicated

band of bomb makers—skilled scientists and technicians in possession of plutonium—might fashion "a modestly effective implosion bomb." Alternatively, such a group might choose to use its plutonium in a technically simpler radiation dispersal device; the plutonium would be transformed into an aerosol of finely divided particles that could be distributed uniformly into the intake of a large office building's air conditioning system. According to Willrich and Taylor, only 3.5 ounces of this extraordinarily toxic substance (its toxicity is at least 20,000 times that of cobra venom or potassium cyanide) would pose a lethal hazard to everyone in the building.

Uninhibited Terrorists

Terrorist groups in the Middle East today no longer operate according to a code of honor that distinguishes between combatants and non-combatants. Engaged in what Michael Walzer describes as "total war against nations, ethnic groups, and religions," their seething anger is vented almost randomly. As a result, the traditional terrorist methods of political killing or assassination have given way in the Middle East to such indiscriminate forms of terrorism as the killing of Israeli athletes and schoolchildren, the massacre of Christian passengers at an Israeli airport, the commando annihilation of a small hotel in Tel Aviv, and the explosion of bombs in Jerusalem.

The Palestinian terrorists have no inhibitions against the application of maximum force to virtually any segment of human population other than their own. They apparently perceive themselves as engaged in a "no holds barred" situation; the amount of suffering they can inflict is apparently limited only by the availability of weapons.

The word *fedayeen* means self-sacrificers. It is a meaning that must be taken seriously; Palestinian terrorist groups often place a higher value on the achievement of certain political and social objectives than they do their own lives. Consequently, such groups are insensitive to the kinds of threats of retaliatory destruction that lie at the heart of the principle of deterrence. Faced with a new kind of international actor for whom the "deadly logic" of deterrence is immobilized, states bent upon counter-terrorist measures are at a unique disadvantage.

This can be illustrated most dramatically by several spectacular "special operations" conducted by the PFLP and the exploits within Al Fatah of Black September. Indeed, the general experience of PFLP commandos is death, either in combat on their expeditions or by their own hand. Only sixteen to twenty-two years old, these terrorists often intentionally detonate their explosive-crammed belts on completion of a mission.

What are the implications of this type of behavior for the threat of nuclear terrorism in the Middle East? If Palestinian terrorists were to obtain nuclear weapons and calculate the prospective costs and benefits of their use, the fear of retaliatory destruction would probably be excluded from their calculation. Orthodox threats of deterrence, therefore, would have no bearing on the terrorists' decision whether or not to use nuclear weapons. If diplomatic or other forms of persuasion are unsuccessful, the threatened nuclear act could be prevented only by a "surgical" or pre-emptive strike.

Heightening the threat of nuclear terrorism in the Middle East is the growing cooperation among terrorist groups. Such cooperation is indicated by the weapons training of Venezuelan terrorist Ilitch Ramirez Sanchez in Lebanon by the PFLP; the weapons training of the Japanese Red Army movement in Lebanon; the establishment of joint training programs and arms transfers between the Turkish People's Army and Black September; and the training of United States Weathermen, Irish Republican Army members, and representatives of Nicaragua's *Tandanista* movement in Palestinian camps. Additional evidence of terrorist collaboration can be detected in the demand by Black September operatives in Munich for the release of

German insurgents who had been involved in killings of German policemen.

Perhaps the most notorious example of cooperation involving operatives in the Middle East is the relationship between the PFLP and the Japanese Red Army. It was this terrorist alliance that brought on the Lydda Airport massacre at Tel Aviv in May 1972. There, three members of the Red Army—trained in fedayeen camps and provided with false passports by PFLP agents—killed 26 persons and wounded 80.

The recent Red Army attack on the American embassy offices in Kuala Lumpur points to a continuing link between the two groups. In the interval between the 1972 airport venture and the Kuala Lumpur attack, mixed Red Army-PFLP squads hijacked a JAL plane (in July 1973) and attacked the Japanese embassy in Kuwait (in February 1974). In September 1974, a Red Army group commandeered the French embassy at The Hague and obtained the release of both PFLP and Red Army agents.

Terrorist cooperation greatly increases the opportunities for terrorists to acquire nuclear weapons, especially when acquisition takes the form of the development and design of nuclear weapons from "raw" fissionable materials. Cooperation among terrorist groups is likely to facilitate the proliferation of "private" nuclear weapons throughout the world, creating a network in which such weapons can be exchanged and transmitted with impunity across national frontiers. Cooperation among terrorists is also apt to spread the benefits of training in the use of nuclear weapons, and to provide such reciprocal privileges as forged documents, which can ease the penetration of and retreat from target areas, and safe havens, which are essential for pre-attack preparations and post-attack security.

Greater Tolerance of Terrorism

It is a curious fact of modern political life that while terrorists are engaged in "total war" with nations, religions, and ethnic groups, the prevailing global attitude is one of tolerance, even permissiveness. In the case of the Palestine Liberation Movement, unqualified applications of violence have even spawned political recognition. Most dramatically, this tolerance provides a spectacular opportunity for groups like Fatah and PFLP to increase their strength and to step up their activities with little fear of interference. The tolerance of terrorism may pave the way for a nuclear weapons capability on the part of the terrorists.

Unless the possibility of terrorist use of nuclear weapons is quickly eliminated, there may be immeasurable calamity in the Middle East. To prevent this, governments can take decisive measures to ensure against the theft of assembled weapons from military stockpiles and fissionable materials from the nuclear energy industry. Some steps in this direction are now being taken by the United States at military and industrial levels; but worldwide efforts must be undertaken to implement such essential safeguards as heavy containers, vaults, barriers, locks, alarms, remote surveillance, and armed guards. New and more imaginative protection systems can also be explored. One promising area involves the utilization of quick-hardening plastic foam which is effectively impenetrable and can be sprayed into storage vaults in case of attack.

Since the safeguards of nuclear materials must be international, the full weight of diplomacy must be brought to bear. The Treaty on the Non-Proliferation of Nuclear Weapons (NPT), which entered into force on March 5, 1970, appears the most probable source of diplomatic procedures. Regrettably, on the basis of what is known about the status of treaties in general and the Non-Proliferation Treaty in particular, there is little cause for optimism, because the IAEA (International Atomic Energy Agency), associated with the NPT, represents neither an effective instrument of international enforcement nor a viable mechanism of international inspection.

Even more disconcerting is the fact that all such measures

suffer from a particularly glaring defect; they offer a technological response to what is manifestly a human problem. As Mason Willrich has observed, there is no reliable "technological fix" when the problem is one of "safeguarding nuclear materials in a world of malfunctioning people." What is needed, then, is a strategy to strengthen the fragile partnership of technological safeguards and diplomatic processes.

Diplomatic processes must block the cooperation of various terrorist groups and must reject all terrorist demands. In the absence of such international action, the threat of nuclear terrorism is very real.

INTERNATIONAL TERRORISM: A SURVEY [5]

What precisely is "international terrorism"? It has three characteristics.

First, as with other forms of terrorism, it embodies an act which is essentially criminal. It takes the form of assassination or murder, kidnapping, extortion, arson, maiming, or an assortment of other acts which are commonly regarded by all nations as criminal.

Second, international terrorism is politically motivated. An extremist political group, convinced of the rightness of its cause, resorts to violent means to advance that cause—means incorporating one of the acts I have just cited. Often the violence is directed against innocents, persons having no personal connection with the grievance motivating the terrorist act.

And *third,* international terrorism transcends national boundaries, through the choice of a foreign victim or target, commission of the terrorist act in a foreign country, or

[5] Excerpts from "International Terrorism," address by Robert A. Fearey made at Los Angeles, California, on February 19, 1976, before the Los Angeles World Affairs Council and the World Affairs Council of Orange County. Mr. Fearey was special assistant to the Secretary of State and Coordinator for Combatting Terrorism, 1975-1976. *Department of State Bulletin.* 74:394-403. Mr. 29, '76.

effort to influence the policies of a foreign government. The international terrorist strikes abroad or at a diplomat or other foreigner at home, because he believes he can thereby exert the greatest possible pressure on his own or another government or on world opinion.

The international terrorist may or may not wish to kill his victim or victims. In abduction or hostage-barricade cases he usually does not wish to kill—though he often will find occasion to do so at the outset to enhance the credibility of his threats. In other types of attacks innocent deaths are his specific, calculated, pressure-shock objective. Through brutality and fear he seeks to impress his existence and his cause on the minds of those who can, through action or terror-induced inaction, help him to achieve that cause.

An example: On September 6, 1970, the Popular Front for the Liberation of Palestine hijacked three airliners flying from Europe to New York, diverted them to airports in the Middle East, and moments after their passengers had been evacuated, blew them up. The terrorists' purposes were:

☐ to attract world attention to the Palestinian cause

☐ to convince the world that the Palestinians could not be ignored in a Middle East settlement or there would be no lasting settlement

☐ to demonstrate that they had destructive powers which they were prepared to use, not just against Israel but far afield against other governments and peoples, until their aims were achieved.

Another recent and vivid example: Last December 21 [1975], five professional international terrorists—a Venezuelan, two Palestinians, and two Germans—took control of the OPEC [Organization of Petroleum Exporting Countries] ministers and their staffs in Vienna, killing three persons in the process, demanded and received publicity for their "Arab rejectionist" cause over the Austrian national radio, and finally released the last of their understandably shaken hostages in Algeria. [See preceding article for information on Arab Rejection Front.—Ed.] Their purpose appears to have been to pressure the more moderate Middle East governments into tougher oil and anti-Israel policies.

Historical Origin

Terrorism as a form of violence for political ends is as old as history, probably older. It is said to have acquired its modern name from the French Reign of Terror of the mid-1790s. The first use of international terrorism is hard to pinpoint. However, the historians among you will recall the Moroccan rebel Raisuli's kidnapping of an American and an Englishman in 1904 in a successful attempt to force the United States and British governments to pressure France into compelling the Sultan of Morocco to comply with Raisuli's ransom, prisoner-release, and other demands. [For further discussion of origins of terrorism see "Terrorism: Origins and Strategy," in Section I, above.]

Perhaps the opening phase of the international terrorist threat we face today, though itself a reaction to oppression and terror, was the hijackings by freedom-seeking escapees from the East European Communist countries in the middle and late forties. In the early sixties the stream of hijackings from the United States to Cuba commenced. Terrorist groups around the world saw the potential for publicity in hijackings and began to use them for attention-getting political objectives. Beginning in about 1968, Palestinian and other violence-oriented political groups in several parts of the world began to extend their terrorist activities to countries—or to the diplomats of countries—not directly involved in the dispute giving rise to the violence.

Modern Terrorism

The years since 1968 have seen a progressive development of the employment of international terrorism for the attainment of national, ethnic, or world revolutionary political goals. They have also seen a marked development of intelligence, training, financial, and operational collaboration among terrorist groups in different parts of the world. And they have seen such groups take increasingly telling advantage of technological advances which afford the terrorist opportunities he never had before:

Air Transport. Two or three individuals can take control of a large airplane with 200–300 passengers, divert it wherever they wish, and blow it up when they get there, with or without its passengers aboard. Or a loaded aircraft can be downed by a bomb placed in its hold. Little wonder that the airplane has figured in so many terrorist acts of the last fifteen years.

Communications. Today's television, radio, and press enable a terrorist to achieve an almost instantaneous horrified, attention-riveted audience for his action. Since public attention to his cause is usually one of his key objectives, communications advances have been critically valuable to the terrorist.

Weapons. New types of weapons are constantly adding to terrorists' capabilities. A leading example: the Soviet SA-7 heat-seeking rocket, equivalent of our Red Eye, easily portable by one man, capable of bringing down commercial aircraft. Two of these weapons were found in the hands of Arab terrorists at the end of a runway in Rome in 1973; fortunately they were found in time. Another key terrorist weapon: plastic explosives.

Targets. Finally, our complex and interdependent modern world society presents a plethora of vulnerable, damaging targets for terrorists. Large aircraft are one such target. But there are also supertankers, electric power grids, gaslines, nuclear power plants, and others. Modern terrorists can cause destruction far beyond anything possible in earlier, simpler ages.

The US Response

So beginning about 1968, our government faced a clear problem of terrorist use of aircraft, of modern communications media, of powerful light-weight precision weapons, and of cooperation among terrorist groups in different countries, all to achieve political shock effects in an increasingly interdependent and vulnerable world. The danger grew, with a mounting series of kidnappings, bombings, murders, and shoot-outs, by Palestinians, Croatians, Tupamaros, Cubans, Turks, and others. In September 1972, eleven Israeli athletes were killed, along with five terrorists, at the Munich Olympic games before an appalled TV audience of hundreds of millions.

Our government had until that time pursued a number of antiterrorist efforts, mainly in the hijacking area. But with Munich, President Nixon and Secretary of State Rogers decided to adopt a more systematic approach. The President directed Secretary Rogers to chair a Cabinet Committee to Combat Terrorism and also to establish an operating arm of the Committee called the Cabinet Committee Working Group. The Working Group originally consisted of senior representatives of the ten Cabinet Committee members, but twelve other agencies concerned with different aspects of terrorism have since been added.

The Cabinet Committee and Working Group have a broad mandate to devise and implement the most effective possible means to combat terrorism at home and abroad. The Cabinet Committee meets as required, and the Working Group has met 101 times. It is the coordinating forum for the entire United States government antiterrorism effort. When a terrorist abduction of an American abroad or of a foreigner in the United States occurs, we set up and run a task force in the State Department's Operations Center. A similar, complementary task force is established in the concerned US Embassy abroad. We have, unfortunately, gained considerable experience in coping with such incidents after hostage cases in Port-au-Prince, Khartoum, Guadalajara, Córdoba, Santo Domingo, Kuala Lumpur, Beirut, and other places.

Means of Combating Terrorism

What have we learned from our study of terrorism and from our practical experience with it? How does one combat terrorism? Basically in three ways:

Intelligence. If you can learn his plans ahead of time, you can sometimes forestall the terrorist. It was through intelligence that the terrorists armed with SA-7's were apprehended at the edge of the airport in Rome before they could destroy their intended Israeli Airlines target. The CIA, the FBI, and other intelligence agencies coordinate their antiterrorist efforts through the Cabinet Committee Working Group.

Physical Security of Target Installations and People. Here again, we have improved our position significantly since 1972. US civil airport security has been strengthened to the point where, in combination with bilateral and multilateral antihijacking conventions, we have not had a successful commercial hijacking in the United States in three years—though there was, of course, the terrible bombing . . . [in December 1975] at La Guardia [New York City]. The security of our diplomatic posts abroad has been upgraded with armored limousines, more marine guards, closed-circuit TV systems, careful briefing of personnel, et cetera.

Apprehension and Punishment of Terrorists. To achieve this key objective we seek international cooperation. The threat is international and can be met only by international means. A major focus of US effort and initiative with other nations has been in the antihijacking area. We took the lead in negotiating in the International Civil Aviation Organization three conventions on hijacking and aircraft sabotage. The general idea of all these conventions, now ratified or adhered to by about seventy countries, is to deter terrorists by internationalizing their criminal acts and thus providing legal means of apprehending and punishing them.

But we have not been altogether successful in this purpose. Hijacking has declined sharply, but more because of improved airport security than the antihijacking conventions—except for our highly effective bilateral agreement with Cuba. [The agreement expired in early 1977.—Ed.] Too few countries are willing to arrest, try, and severely punish international hijackers and saboteurs, or indeed international terrorists of any kind. US efforts for the adoption of enforcement mechanisms to give the international aircraft-hijacking and sabotage conventions sanctions teeth, by denying air services to noncomplying countries, have been completely unavailing. A US-proposed convention in the 1972 UN General Assembly which would have obliged participating states to prosecute or extradite international terrorists coming under their control, at safe haven destinations or in other ways, won the support of only about half a dozen nations. It did, however, serve as the genesis of the UN convention to protect diplomats and foreign officials, adopted in 1973 but still awaiting the necessary ratifications to come into effect.

The Rand Corporation recently calculated, on the basis of experience since 1968, that there is an 80 percent chance that an international terrorist involved in a kidnapping will escape death or capture. The terrorist kidnapper has a close to even chance that all or some of his ransom demands will be granted. Worldwide publicity, normally an important terrorist objective, is achieved in almost every case. For all crimes of terrorism (as opposed to just kidnapping), the average sentence for the small proportion of terrorists caught and tried is less than eighteen months.

In a word, outside the hijacking area, our and a small but, hopefully, growing number of other governments' efforts to make terrorism unprofitable for the terrorists have made little headway.

So these are the ways we seek to combat terrorism: intelligence, physical security, and apprehension and punishment of terrorists. In addition, and very importantly, we encourage and assist other nations to alleviate the inequities and frustrations from which international terrorism mainly—though by no means entirely—arises. Unfortunately, effective action to reduce these inequities and frustrations is in many instances a very long-term proposition. The trend in most countries and regions is the other way. The awakening political consciousness of oppressed, poverty-stricken, or otherwise frustrated peoples on every continent threatens an increasing resort to terrorism in areas now relatively free of it. . . .

The United States has not yet had to face seizures or attacks within its own territories by international terrorist groups. Would our government, as a host government responsible for dealing with such incidents at home, practice the same firm no-concessions policies it has urged on other governments, including when our own citizens have been abducted abroad?

The answer is yes. We are convinced of the soundness of these policies. And we have seen other governments, faced with a series of terrorist incidents of a type we have thus far been spared, arrive by hard experience at the conclusion that firmness is the only course. We have dealt as firmly as the law allows with domestic terrorist organizations, such as the Black Panthers, Symbionese Liberation Army, Weather Underground, and Puerto Rican Liberation Armed Force. I do not think you will find your government wanting if, unhappily, the international terrorist menace reaches our shores.

I have discussed the international terrorist threat and the US response to that threat. What are the principal issues and requirements as we look to the future?

International Cooperation Against Terrorists

First, how are we to achieve more effective international cooperation for the apprehension, trial, and punishment of international terrorists?

This objective is as intractable as it is central. Most

countries apparently remain unwilling to apply strict legal sanctions to international terrorists. In the Third World, where most of the difficulty lies, many countries sympathize with the political aspirations of groups which practice terrorism. There is the sympathy of Arab governments for the Palestinian cause, including approval of terrorist attacks on Israel and, in the case of the radical Arab governments, approval and support of Palestinian terrorist attacks in Europe and elsewhere as well. There is the sympathy of newly independent countries, many of which used terrorism to help achieve their freedom, for anticolonial terrorist groups. And there is the sympathy of practically all Third World governments for terrorists striking against repressive authoritarian regimes, particularly in the developed world. Third World governments generally accept the terrorists' argument that the weak and oppressed, with their pleas for justice unheeded, and lacking the means for conventional war, have no alternative to terrorism—that terrorism in a perceived "just" cause is not criminal but patriotic and heroic.

We, with our Judeo-Christian tradition, can understand this reasoning up to a point, but we can never accept it. We believe there can be no justification, in any circumstances, for the deliberate killing of innocent individuals. We recognize that the alternatives to terrorism, centering on peaceful protest, constructive proposals, and negotiation, often involve frustration and delay. But we believe that, in an interdependent world attempting to move away from violence before it is too late, they offer the only acceptable means of change.

For different reasons than those put forward by Third World countries, most advanced countries are also disinclined to commit themselves to clear and unequivocal sanctions against terrorists. Sometimes they are inhibited by political or commercial interests from offending governments that support or condone terrorism. Or they are concerned that if they convict and imprison terrorists this will attract more terrorists to their territories seeking, through further violence, to free their comrades. Or they are reluctant to see rights of political asylum weakened. The Communist giants, the Soviet Union and China, appear to share our conviction that hijacking, aircraft sabotage, and other forms of international terrorism are a criminal threat to civilized society and should be stopped. But they also share the Third World's belief that terrorism as an instrument of "wars of national liberation" is acceptable, and they support such terrorism. . . .

Effectiveness of Terrorism

A second question: How effective has international terrorism been for the terrorists' purposes?

Clearly, international terrorists have had tactical successes, as recently at Kuala Lumpur and Vienna, achieving their objectives of publication or broadcasting of manifestos, release of imprisoned comrades, or extortion of ransom. And these successes have been achieved at small cost to the terrorists—most have escaped to safe havens, or, if caught, have later been rescued by comrades or served very short terms. On the other hand, international terrorist groups have fruitlessly suffered suicidal losses in attacks within Israel. And such groups operating in Europe and elsewhere have in a number of cases suffered heavy casualties while achieving none of their purposes, except dubious publicity, as in the Baader-Meinhof seizure of the German Embassy in Stockholm last April [1975]. . . .

How about terrorist groups' attainment of their fundamental political goals—the causes their abductions and attacks are intended to serve?

Here, too, the overall record is hardly a source of encouragement for terrorists. Certainly the Baader-Meinhof Gang and the Japan Red Army have not succeeded in advancing their nihilist, world revolution cause significantly. The kidnappings and murders of US and other diplomats in Brazil, Guatemala, Argentina, and elsewhere have won the

terrorists no discernible political gains. The terrorism perpetrated by South Moluccan extremists in the Netherlands
achieved world publicity, as sensational crimes are wont to
do. But the terrorism was essentially negative in its consequences for the South Moluccan cause, embarrassing the
group's responsible members and outraging the Netherlands
government and people.

As for Palestinian terrorism, the Palestinian cause is unquestionably more widely known as a result of Palestinian
terrorism than it otherwise would be. But against this must
be set the revulsion of all civilized peoples over the crimes
committed by Palestinian terrorist groups at Lod, Munich,
Khartoum, within Israel, and elsewhere. And terrorist attacks have contributed importantly to the hatred and bitterness which impede a Middle East settlement from which
the Palestinians might hope to achieve their goal of a Palestinian state. The decline in Palestinian terrorism within
the past two years suggests that the more moderate Palestinian leaders have come in part, at least, to share the view
that terrorism is counterproductive to the attainment of
Palestinian objectives.

International terrorism, in short, is no success story, for
the Palestinians, the South Moluccans, or any other group.

Seriousness as a World Problem

A third question, then, is: How deeply need we be concerned about international terrorism as a world problem?

Up to now international terrorism's toll in dead and
wounded and property damage has been relatively small.
This is true of all forms of terrorism, compared with the casualties and property losses of even the most minor conventional wars. But it is particularly true of international terrorism. It has been estimated that some eight hundred
people have been killed, including terrorists, and some
seventeen hundred injured, in all international terrorist
incidents from 1968 through the present. Year by year this
is no more than the crime rate of one moderate-sized Amer-

ican city, intolerably high as that rate is. Property damage, principally in destroyed aircraft, has been equally limited.

But international terrorism's limited toll in lives and property thus far is only part of the story. There are a number of things we should note and ponder:

☐ Most of the world's airports are now manned by guards and inspectors, aided where possible by expensive X-ray machines. Even so, no air traveler is secure from terrorist attack.

☐ US and other nations' embassies in Beirut, Buenos Aires, Nicosia, and many other capitals are heavily guarded, in sharp contrast with, and derogation of, their diplomatic function. Diplomats can no longer go about their business in any capital without varying degrees of fear of being kidnapped or killed.

☐ The world's leading statesmen work and travel under costly and inhibiting restrictions.

☐ Mail received at potential target addresses, such as my own government department, must be X-rayed for explosives before delivery.

☐ State authority is weakened as government's accede to terrorist demands for release of prisoners, ransom, and publicity.

☐ The principles and standards of justice are impaired as the perpetrators of horrible acts of violence are given short sentences or let free.

None of these conditions has reached critical proportions. But in combination they signal a potential for mounting, serious erosion of world order if we do not succeed in bringing the international terrorist threat under control.

Future of Terrorism

So, finally, what of the future?

I just noted terrorism's, particularly international terrorism's, relatively small toll in killed and wounded and property damage. This could soon begin to change. New weapons are constantly enlarging terrorists' destructive capabilities.

Particularly rapid advances are being made in individual weapons development as we and other advanced nations seek to equip our foot soldiers with increased, highly accurate firepower. There is obvious risk of growing quantities of these weapons coming into the hands of terrorists, weapons which are as capable of being employed against civil aircraft, supertankers, motorcades, and speakers' podiums as against military targets. The Soviet SA-7 heat-seeking, man-portable missile has already, as I mentioned, been found in the hands of terrorists.

And there are more serious hazards. As nuclear power facilities multiply, the quantity and geographical dispersion of plutonium and other fissionable materials in the world will increase greatly. The possibility of credible nuclear terrorist threats based on illicitly constructed atomic bombs, stolen nuclear weapons, or sabotage of nuclear power installations can be expected to grow. Even more plausible would be threats based on more readily and economically produced chemical and biological agents, such as nerve gas and pathogenic bacteria.

Would terrorists actually use such weapons? Probably not. They could already have attacked cities with toxic aerosols, for example, but have not done so. Terrorists, at least the rational ones, fundamentally seek to influence people, not kill them. The death of thousands, or tens of thousands, of persons could produce a tremendous backlash against those responsible and their cause. But the possibility of credible nuclear, chemical, and biological threats, particularly by anarchists, is real. Though the chances of such threats being carried out may be small, the risk is there and must be met.

There is a further danger—one of international terrorist groups for hire, which we may already be seeing in an incipient stage. A government might employ such groups to attack, alarm, or subvert another government or interna-

tional organization. Powerful pressures might be brought
to bear through a small, deniable expenditure by the aggressor government.

The future, some believe, holds a prospect of reduced
resort to open warfare but of a high level of subversive and
terroristic violence and insecurity originating with governments or subgovernmental elements using, or threatening to
use, against our vulnerable modern societies, the frightening
small, or even more frightening mass-effect, weapons I have
cited. A world of many Ulsters might be statistically safer
for the average man than the world of the past sixty years
of repeated major conflicts. But it would be a more nerve-
wracking and unsettled world of continuing low-level violence and threatened mass-destruction terrorist attack.

TERRORISM IN THE UNITED STATES [6]

Reprinted from *U.S. News & World Report.*

The arrests of Patricia Hearst and the last self-pro-
claimed members of the Symbionese Liberation Army are
not the end of US terrorist gangs.

But, for many underground fugitives, the "big bust" in
San Francisco may well mark the beginning of the end.

"The word is out," said one high-ranking investigator,
"and every terrorist in the country is sweating, waiting for
that knock on the door."

In addition, sympathizers who have been hiding the terrorists now are expected to have second thoughts about the
penalties they might face.

Such optimistic expectations were typical of state and
federal authorities eager to dig into the huge store of evidence found at the hideaways of Miss Hearst and her fellow
suspects, William and Emily Harris. On September 24
[1975], this optimism was backed up by a pre-dawn FBI raid
in Seattle, Washington, that nabbed Leonard Handelsman,

[6] From "Drive to Root Out U.S. Terror Gangs." *U.S. News & World Report.*
69:22. O. 6, '75.

a founder of the nation's premier terrorist group, the Weather Underground.

Investigators believe that the hottest leads to the network sheltering dozens of underground terrorists may come from questioning the SLA suspects themselves.

On September 23, Miss Hearst avoided cross-examination in a bail-reduction hearing—at least temporarily—when her lawyers claimed that her mental condition was "too fragile" because of brainwashing and torture by the SLA. The judge said he would rule on that question after an examination by court-appointed psychiatrists. . . .

In an affidavit, the publishing heiress swore that she was kept in a closet for more than two months until she was ordered to take part in a San Francisco bank robbery in April 1974—which the government claims marked her "conversion" to the SLA. But the affidavit said that she was forced into the robbery at gunpoint and made tape recordings denouncing her family only under threats of death from her captors. Miss Hearst has no clear memory of her actions since the holdup . . ., according to the sworn statement. . . .

The Harrises, too, refused to talk. But pressure mounted when the couple was taken to Los Angeles to face eighteen state charges—including kidnapping and assault with intent to murder. The felony counts stemmed from a shooting spree at a sporting-goods store the day before six SLA members died in a Los Angeles gun battle in May 1974.

Cracking the Underground

The sudden signs of FBI success gave rise to reports that the agency was finally getting informers who could crack the hard shell of closeness and trust that had protected the radicals over such a long period.

And investigation of fringe figures in the Hearst case was putting pressure on supporters with relatively clean records to start talking, authorities said.

Moreover, the weapons found in the SLA's San Francisco apartments were being studied for possible links with other

California crimes—including the shotgun slaying of a woman in a bank robbery last April [1975] and the apparent executions of a radical prison reformer and a female teacher last June [1975]. Scores of captured documents also were said to point the way toward surviving groups that make up the bulk of American terrorism.

One of the first targets: a shadowy group of perhaps twenty terrorists which has been blamed for dozens of bombings along the West Coast under such names as New World Liberation Front, Red Guerrilla Family and George Jackson Brigade. One such blast, which injured nine people in a supermarket in Seattle, Washington, . . . was said to be in retaliation for the Hearst arrest the same day. Law officers there were trying to determine whether their new prisoner, Leonard Handelsman, might have been involved, and whether his arrest would provide a link with their main target, the Weather Underground. . . .

Other active terrorist groups include the Black Liberation Army, described as a splinter from California's now-peaceful Black Panther Party, and a Puerto Rican organization called the Army Forces of National Liberation, which claimed credit for the deaths of four people in a tavern explosion in New York City last January [1975].

Nationwide, the FBI reports 1,178 bombing incidents in the first seven months of 1975, 56 more than during the same period last year. Bombing deaths totaled 31 and injuries 206—more than double the 1974 rate.

Although the number of actual bombers and killers is small, the FBI says that thousands of sympathizers have been willing to shelter them—at least until now. An investigator who has spent years pursuing these terrorists said: "We try not to get excited at a break like this, because we've just missed catching the big leaders so many times before. But the heat is definitely on now, and it will be interesting to see the results."

III. DOES TERRORISM PAY?

EDITOR'S INTRODUCTION

Can there be any moral justification for an act of terrorism? Would the death of a Hitler or a Stalin at the hands of a terrorist have served mankind well or ill? Rare is the terrorist who fails to view his cause as just or his morality as superior to that of the world around him. And even the advocates of the sternest counterterrorist measures concede that the alleviation of legitimate grievances is one of the requisites to reversing the terrorist trend.

Yet acts of terrorism, though they may draw attention to a cause and even gain it a measure of political recognition, do not serve to ensure the success of the cause. On the contrary, as Palestinian terrorists have found, such acts succeed mainly in arousing public indignation. As the distinguished political observer Walter Laqueur has pointed out, terrorism is above all an act of futility and as such even the moral worth of the cause being advocated is compromised by the means employed.

Cause and motivation are the subject of this section. In the first article Jeffrey A. Tannenbaum, a reporter for the *Wall Street Journal*, briefly summarizes the impetus to terrorism around the world. Next, Neil Hickey of *TV Guide* discusses the role of the media—particularly television—in instigating terrorist acts. The reader who has pondered this matter may be relieved to know that it is also being carefully considered in TV newsrooms around the country.

Writers for the *New Republic* debate the moral justification for terrorism in the third article, and in the last article in this section Walter Laqueur sets forth a number of terrorist myths and emphasizes the political ineffectiveness of terrorism. He concludes: "Compared with other dangers threatening mankind, it is almost irrelevant."

GAINING POLITICAL RECOGNITION [1]

With horrifying regularity, the tableau is played out upon the world stage. A random bomb, a machine gun fired into an unsuspecting crowd, a pirated aircraft touching down in one major capital after another. Through it all, headlines and television films chronicle the terrorist's latest exploits for the watching world.

For almost a decade, a few politically motivated killers have successfully managed to inject themselves into world politics, practicing a form of psychological warfare on a grand scale.

Disparate in their political aims, aligned only in their tactics, these terrorists have won a notoriety and influence far exceeding their numbers or actual deeds. The State Department's Office for Combatting Terrorism lists 737 terrorist acts resulting in 292 deaths from the beginning of 1973 through October 1976. This toll is "pathetic and puny" compared to other forms of violence, says H. H. A. Cooper, professor of law and psychiatry at American University. As just one example, over 20,000 Americans were homicide victims in 1975 alone.

Yet terrorism has enormous visceral impact—and, by extension, political influence. The dramatic, impersonal nature of most terrorist attacks, the frequent choice of civilian targets and the willingness to export violence to any place where the publicity payoff is apt to be great, make the terrorist's deeds especially chilling. Like the psychopathic killer, the terrorist is "likely to attack anybody," says Nicholas N. Kittrie, director of the Institute for Advanced Studies in Justice at American University. But unlike the aberrant, lone psychopath, a terrorist has followers who, it is reasoned, are likely to strike again.

Indeed, the phenomenon is contagious; any ragtag group with a few rifles and enough daring can garner in-

[1] From "For World's Alienated, Violence Often Reaps Political Recognition," by Jeffrey A. Tannenbaum, staff reporter. *Wall Street Journal.* 189:1+. Ja. 4, '77. Reprinted with permission of the *Wall Street Journal* © 1977 Dow Jones & Company Inc. All Rights Reserved.

stant recognition for a hitherto-obscure cause. Most terrorists seem satisfied with such short-term gains. According to Ambassador L. Douglas Heck, [former] director of the Office for Combatting Terrorism, the record shows that terrorists have an 80 percent chance of escaping death or capture, a 50 percent chance of having some or all of their immediate demands met, and "a 100 percent chance of getting all the publicity sought."

In at least this narrow sense, then, terrorism pays. And as a result, many experts expect that terrorist tactics will be adopted by increasing numbers of disaffected groups as time goes by. "Terrorism is going to grow rather than lessen," says Yonah Alexander, professor of international studies at the State University of New York and a frequent lecturer on terrorism. "Today," he adds, "we are entering an Age of Terror."

These same experts are quick to note that for the moment at least, terrorist activity has plateaued. In the past two years, no sharp upsurge in the number of incidents has been noted, in contrast to steady increases in previous years. One possible cause for the leveling off: The Palestine Liberation Organization, which authorities hold responsible for about a fifth of all terrorist incidents in the past five years, has been bogged down in the Lebanese civil war since early 1975.

For the long term, however, authorities marshal a persuasive case that terrorism will grow and become more dangerous. "The world will witness steadily greater and more widespread sophistication in terrorist targeting, execution and weaponry," warns a report released last April [1976] by the Central Intelligence Agency.

Indeed, the spread of television and communications satellites makes it easier for terrorists to achieve instant, worldwide publicity. Today's vast computer centers and nuclear power plants represent tempting—and vulnerable—targets for those wishing to paralyze large population centers in a single stroke. And certain new weapons seem almost tailor-made for the terrorist. Small, portable guided missiles like the United States' Redeye and the Soviet's Strela give even one person immense destructive power. As these weapons spread, analysts say, it's inevitable that more of them will find their way into terrorists' hands.

In the Ascendancy

At the same time, political currents that tend to breed terrorism are in the ascendancy around the globe. Separatist and revolutionary movements are multiplying, as the power of nation-states to hold together diverse minorities diminishes. The Irish in Great Britain, the Basques in Spain, the Croatians in Yugoslavia, the Puerto Ricans in the United States: Over a dozen nations face violence by separatist groups such as these. And within the borders of some twenty other countries—including West Germany, Argentina and Burma—are active guerrilla groups "with revolutionary as opposed to separatist aims," according to a recent Rand Corporation report prepared for the State Department.

Who are the terrorists? Authorities estimate that throughout the world, between 1,000 and 3,000 people live "underground," working for one of perhaps fifty different revolutionary or separatist groups known to practice terrorist tactics. Among the most active at the moment: the Provisional Wing of the Irish Republican Army, Argentine Montonero revolutionaries and anti-Castro Cubans based in the United States. Most of the known terrorist groups confine their activities to their homelands. But a growing number are taking their violence outside their own countries; they are known as "international" or "transnational" terrorists.

Most terrorists don't fit the wild-eyed "mad bomber" stereotype. Though extremist groups do attract psychopaths, most terrorists are coolly rational, even conventional people. According to Irving Louis Horowitz, professor of sociology at Rutgers University, terrorists are usually young (aged twenty to thirty-five), middle-class, relatively well-educated and are performing their terrorist duties "as an avocation." For example, the man who founded the Popular Front for the Liberation of Palestine and subsequently gained world attention for a series of airline hijackings and explosions is George Habash, a physician who was trained at the American University in Beirut.

One element that all terrorist groups have in common is military and political weakness—even desperation—and the need to take dramatic steps to give the appearance of strength. Brian M. Jenkins, a Rand Corporation analyst, writes that terrorists "hope to persuade other nations to pressure their adversary into a settlement more favorable to the terrorists' cause than the terrorists themselves could achieve."

Their inherent weakness helps explain why terrorists often attack innocent third parties or foreign targets. In Iran, for example, tight security makes it difficult for the Shah's enemies to operate, although they did manage the murders last August [1976] of three Rockwell International Corporation employees associated with a government project. Analysts expect that increasingly, the Shah's enemies will choose targets outside Iran. Terrorists "will always take the path of least resistance," one analyst says.

But if terror is a potent weapon for the weak, it can also backfire for an established group. Pro-Palestinian guerrillas hurt their cause, most experts agree, when they raided the Vienna meeting of the Organization of Petroleum Exporting Countries in December 1975. The incident, which was disavowed by the PLO [Palestine Liberation Organization], marked the first time that Palestinians had turned against Arabs, their principal backers.

Earlier, of course, the PLO had successfully used terror to gain recognition from the Arab states and a platform at the United Nations, where Yasir Arafat, the PLO leader, was invited to speak in 1974. "Terrorism is an effective way of gathering attention to a cause, but it runs the risk of being counterproductive once it gathers that attention," says Andrew J. Pierre, a political scientist with the Council on Foreign Relations in New York.

Most terrorists seek legitimacy in the eyes of the world

and, analysts say, are keenly aware that too much killing can harm their cause. Indeed, self-restraint by the terrorists themselves may be the key element in controlling their violence, because nations can do little to stop even a few desperate individuals willing to die for a cause. It's widely believed, for example, that terrorists won't try to obtain and explode nuclear weapons, although some groups may attempt to exploit the threat of doing so.

Nevertheless, terrorists appear to be growing more dangerous. Increasingly, there has been evidence of links between different groups in planning and carrying out violence. The guerrillas who raided the Vienna OPEC meeting are said to have been drawn from both the Popular Front for the Liberation of Palestine, a PLO group, and the Baader-Meinhof gang, a West German organization whose leaders have since been killed or jailed but whose activities are being carried out by a successor group. This sort of collusion leads the Rand Corporation's Mr. Jenkins to suggest the possibility that an international terrorist brigade may emerge and "offer itself to all the world's revolutionary movements."

Who Is Carlos?

According to the recent CIA study on terrorism, the reported leader of the Vienna raid, a man known as Carlos, has boasted that he controls "some two score seasoned professionals." Carlos has been identified by the British as Ilitch Ramirez Sanchez, a Venezuelan. He already has been linked to more than one terrorist group. Separately, the tiny (well under fifty members), fanatical Japanese Red Army espouses "simultaneous worldwide revolution." It has allied itself with the Palestinians and apparently is willing to lend guerrillas to other groups.

If more of these "professional terrorists" do step forth, some analysts fear, they may be hired by nations to attack other, enemy states. The ties between some established governments and terrorist groups are already close. The Soviet

Union has trained thousands of soldiers from other countries for "wars of national liberation" in the Mideast, Rhodesia and South Africa. Some of these guerrillas have gone on to become international terrorists, not necessarily under Soviet sponsorship. For its part, the United States armed and trained anti-Castro Cubans in the 1960s, thus laying the groundwork for the anti-Castro terror apparatus that continues today. And the Palestinians depend on the oil-rich Arab nations for financing and sanctuary.

One nation, Libya, is accused by US officials of directly sponsoring terrorists; they cite its harboring of the terrorist Carlos after the raid on the Vienna OPEC meeting. Libya, Iraq, the People's Democratic Republic of Yemen and Somalia, as well as the Soviet Union, are named by the State Department as training areas for terrorists.

If some nations find it in their interest to underwrite terrorists, many others, often because they came into being through revolutionary violence themselves, at least tacitly approve of terrorist activities. It has become almost a cliché in diplomatic circles to note that "one man's terrorist is another man's freedom fighter." This helps explain why, after years of debate, the United Nations has been unable to come up with even a generally satisfactory definition of terrorism, much less a consensus on how to curb it. Since the attack on the Vienna OPEC conference, however, more nations seem ready to take a firmer offensive. The UN General Assembly is expected—possibly this year [1977]—to condemn hostage-taking, a symbolic move that may lead to tougher punishments for terrorists.

Government security officials stress the element of futility involved in trying to guard against the sort of violence that can erupt virtually anywhere in the world. When foiled in one area, terrorists simply switch targets, they note. Thus, when the adoption of rigorous airport security made air hijackings too risky, a wave of attacks on trains, conferences and other less-secure targets erupted. Sometimes elegantly simple security measures can be effective, however.

In Great Britain, letter-bomb incidents fell off sharply after authorities made mailbox slots smaller, and thus less able to accommodate bombs.

The United States State Department has spent $15 million to $19 million a year since 1974 on added protection for its overseas diplomats, and a host of private companies has sprung up to help corporations guard their employees. For example, Pinkerton's Inc. in New York supplies executives overseas with bodyguards, provides a "crisis plan" for dealing with terrorists should the need arise, and offers advice on how the executives can keep a low profile.

Americans: Frequent Targets

US citizens have been victims in one third of all terrorist attacks since 1968, and this country has consistently adopted a hard line with terrorists, refusing to bargain with them or to meet demands. "There would be no end in sight if we started paying ransom every time a United States official was kidnapped—it would be an open invitation to the United States Treasury," says Mr. Heck of the Office for Combatting Terrorism. Critics see this policy as too drastic, and argue that sparing diplomats' lives should take priority over all else. They contend that paying ransom doesn't necessarily encourage more terrorism. One source close to the State Department says that debate on this issue there "is quite heated—there is a lot of bitterness and anger."

Some Western observers worry that the current epidemic of terrorism will lead democracies to invoke repressive countermeasures. The frisking procedures now widely in force at airports may spread to other institutions, they say. According to W. Scott Thompson of the Fletcher School of Law and Diplomacy in Medford, Massachusetts, "Positive identification may soon be needed at all times in most Western societies so that citizens can prove who they are—and more important, who they are not."

Similarly, Professor [Yonah] Alexander of the State University of New York expects stepped-up pressure on the news media for some form of censorship, self-imposed or otherwise, of its coverage of terrorist attacks. David G. Hubbard, a Dallas psychiatrist who has studied dozens of air hijackers, advocates such "restraint" on the part of the media. He says hijackers "are stimulated toward action by news coverage, are educated toward successful crimes by it, and are provided the guaranteed publicity such criminals require before they will act." Others argue that if terrorists were ignored by the press, they would then escalate their violence to new levels of brutality in an effort to seize headlines. In Argentina, it is currently illegal to "publicize" terrorist activities. An interview with leaders of the Montonero guerrillas that was published recently in Spain could not have appeared in Argentina, a United States Information Agency official says.

"Overreaction is more dangerous than the terrorist," cautions J. Bowyer Bell, a researcher at Columbia University's Institute of War and Peace Studies. He and other analysts note that often the repressive measures that are used to crush terrorism remain in force long after the threat of violence has passed. In Uruguay, for example, a military-backed coup threw over an elected government in 1973, during a crisis precipitated by violent activity on the part of the Tupamaro guerrillas. Today, the junta is still firmly entrenched. The Tupamaros have all but disappeared, but so have most civil liberties.

GAINING THE MEDIA'S ATTENTION [2]

"Violence for Effect"

It's called "propaganda of the deed" by experts: violent, criminal acts (often against innocent people) performed by

[2] From "Terrorism and Television: The Medium in the Middle," article in two parts, by Neil Hickey, staff reporter. *TV Guide.* 24:2-6; 10-13. Jl. 31, Ag. 7, '76. Reprinted with permission from TV Guide® Magazine. Copyright © 1976 by Triangle Publications, Inc. Radnor, Pennsylvania.

desperadoes seeking a worldwide forum for their grievances.

More often it's called terrorism; and because such out-bursts are news, they have created a problem for television's news executives: does extensive coverage inspire and in-struct other terrorists or, on the other hand, is censorship of such developments desirable or possible?

Experts are seeking the answers—even as the wave of recent bombings, kidnappings, hijackings, assassinations and commando raids rises to unprecedented levels. Just tune in the television news programs and watch: explosions in London, Belfast and Dublin set off by the Provisional wing of the Irish Republican Army; bombings in New York by Puerto Rican nationalists; the murder of diplomats in Latin America, Europe and Africa; the seizure of embassies in various world capitals; and the machine-gunning of tour-ists in Middle Eastern airports.

In September 1972, eight Palestinian guerrillas broke into the Israeli quarters at the Olympic Games in Munich. In that action and the ensuing clashes with German po-lice—many of which were broadcast live to a dumbstruck world—eleven Israeli athletes were murdered by the guer-rillas and five guerrillas were killed by police. Three guerrillas were caught and later released by the Germans in response to Arabs who hijacked a plane.

In Vienna last December [1975], six pro-Palestinian ter-rorists seized the headquarters of the Organization of Petro-leum Exporting Countries, killed three people and—after forcing Austrian officials to broadcast an anti-Zionist com-muniqué—abducted eleven oil ministers. The kidnappers took their captives on an airborne joy ride to Africa before releasing them unharmed.

On June 17 [1976] United States Ambassador to Leba-non Francis E. Meloy and his economic adviser were shot to death in Beirut. . . . [A few days later] an Air France jet-liner bearing 257 persons was hijacked by pro-Palestinian guerrillas and flown to Uganda in an unsuccessful attempt to force the release of 53 political prisoners. (Israeli commandos freed 103 of the hostages in a daring rescue mission to Uganda.) On July 2, 18 persons were killed and 66 wounded in a bombing at federal police headquarters in Buenos Aires. (In retaliation, right-wing death squads killed 15 people the following day.) Also on July 2, in Boston, 3 bomb blasts—reportedly set off by antibusing groups—destroyed an airliner on the ground, wrecked two National Guard trucks, and badly damaged a suburban courthouse. . . .

In the period from 1965 to the present, almost a thousand incidents of international terrorism have been documented by the United States State Department, the CIA and similar agencies abroad. Since 1968, terrorists have killed more than 800 people and wounded 1,700. But for complex reasons, now being studied by the Rand Corporation and others for the first time, the impact of those crimes on world order is greater than even such figures suggest.

Terrorism as a function of political ideology is not new. From 1881 to 1914, assassins struck down Tsar Alexander II of Russia, President Carnot of France, President McKinley of the United States, and the King of Italy, as well as Archduke Francis Ferdinand, whose death triggered the war [World War I]. Algeria, Spain, Argentina, Turkey, Canada, Cyprus and many other countries were besieged by terrorist violence in the 1950s and 1960s.

But experts report that the flare-up of international violence on the scale we are witnessing today is far more dangerous and potentially disruptive of world peace than anything that has gone before. And they point out that a crucial contributing factor is the global TV coverage that beams terroristic mayhem into the homes of tens of millions in scores of countries.

Impact of TV

Groups like the Tupamaros (Uruguay), the Baader-Meinhof gang (West Germany), the Quebec Liberation Front, the IRA, the United Red Army (Japan), the Eritrean Liberation Front (Ethiopia), separatist units of Basques, Bretons and Corsicans, as well as the many pro-Palestinian activists (and many others) have all absorbed an important lesson of the Supermedia Age: namely, that TV news organizations can be forced into becoming the final link between the terrorist and his audience—if the crime is sufficiently outrageous and dramatic.

When the Baader-Meinhof gang kidnapped a West German politician in February 1975, to force the release from prison of five of their fellows, all of Germany followed the drama on television. The German TV network was, in effect, hijacked and made an accomplice to the crime. Said one German TV editor:

> For seventy-two hours we lost control of the medium. We shifted shows to meet their timetable. [They demanded that] our cameras be in position to record each of the prisoners as they boarded a plane, and our news coverage had to include prepared statements at their dictation. There is plenty of underworld crime on our screens, but up until now Kojak and Columbo were always in charge. Now it was the real thing, and it was the gangsters who wrote the script and programmed the mass media.

Perhaps the most heart-rending aspect of terrorism in the TV age is the "pure terrorism"—the murder, for example, of 26 tourists (and the wounding of 78) at Tel Aviv's Lod International Airport in 1972 by machine-gun-toting Japanese radicals. No longer is it necessary for terrorists to undertake high-risk missions—such as the assassination of heads of state—to achieve their aims. The victims of modern terrorism are most often innocent people and noncombatants, partly because of the guaranteed publicity value of such crimes, and the requirement upon news organizations to report them.

> While terrorists may kill, sometimes wantonly, the primary objective of terrorism is *not* mass murder [says Brian Jenkins, a Rand Corporation expert on terrorism]. Terrorists want a lot of people watching and a lot of people listening, not a lot of people dead.

I see terrorism as violence for effect [he adds]. Terrorists choreograph dramatic incidents to achieve maximum publicity, and in that sense, terrorism is theater.

Terrorist groups tend to be relatively small bands of disaffected outsiders who resort to excessive violence to project themselves as forces to be reckoned with. The Symbionese Liberation Army [SLA], which kidnapped Patricia Hearst, probably never numbered more than a dozen souls. But through their genius for media manipulation, they occupied the nation's attention for most of two years.

Thus, the importance and scope of terrorist groups often undergo what some experts call an "amplification effect" when processed through television (and its journalistic needs). For example: insurgents conducted rural guerrilla warfare in Angola, Mozambique and French Guinea for fifteen years without the world taking much notice. Yet, when a roughly similar number of media-smart Palestinian commandos took their fight from the West Bank desert to the urban centers of Europe and the Middle East—within range of television cameras and reporters—the grievances of stateless Palestinians swiftly became cocktail conversation for TV audiences the world over.

This Palestinian assault on public consciousness through the media reached a triumphal public relations climax when Yasir Arafat, chairman of the Palestine Liberation Organization, became the first spokesman for a nongovernmental group ever to plead his case (in a widely televised address) before the United Nations General Assembly. He has also been interviewed on NBC's *Meet the Press*.

Complicity by the Media?

Serious questions thus are raised about the media's complicity, witting or unwitting, in the current wave of international terrorism. Would the violence decline if television ignored or downplayed it? Does television fan the flames of political terrorism, or foster a contagion? Is self-censorship by TV news organizations a good idea, or even possible, given the competitive climate that exists among them? If television did censor itself, would terrorists merely escalate their outrages until the media simply could *not* ignore them? Is the public's right-to-know absolute? Is TV's right-to-report absolute, or does it have a responsibility for the effects of its reportage? Would modern terrorism exist at all if we did not live on a media-saturated planet? Are there positive steps TV can take to minimize its exploitation by terrorist initiatives?

Observably, many terrorist incidents that are covered routinely in the back pages of newspapers get prominent treatment in TV news broadcasts because of their visual drama and excitement. One expert, Dr. David Hubbard (author of *Skyjacker: His Flights of Fancy*) calls such practices (and especially the live coverage of ongoing terrorist-related events) "social pornography" because it "caters to the sick, unmet needs of the public. Its effect is sedition, whether deliberate or not."

Hubbard is "certain" that world terrorism would decrease if television brought its coverage "down to a level that has some relationship to the importance of the event, which is frequently zero." As a psychiatrist, he has interviewed scores of imprisoned skyjackers and taped hundreds of hours of their reflections. They all say essentially the same thing about the media, he insists: that "they are fools who permit themselves to be used as simply as punching an elevator button." One hijacker, Hubbard reports, stated the terrorists' consensus: "Television is a whore. Any man who wants her full favors can have them in five minutes with a pistol."

Television not only gives terrorism too much air time, says J. Bowyer Bell of Columbia University's Institute of War and Peace Studies, but the medium has become "an essential part of the terrorist exercise: 'Don't shoot, Abdul! We're not on prime time!' I'm not exaggerating at all. They know when satellite time is available. During the OPEC kidnappings in Vienna, the leader of the operation insisted that they stay in the headquarters building long enough for the television cameras to arrive." By taking such groups as the SLA seriously in their own fantasy terms, says Bell, the media invented them as a real political force.

A canvass of other students of terrorism elicits similar convictions:

Dr. Frederick Hacker, a California psychiatrist who has served as negotiator in terrorist incidents: "If the mass media did not exist, terrorists would have to invent them. In turn, the mass media hanker after terroristic acts because they fit into their programming needs: namely, sudden acts of great excitement that are susceptible, presumably, of quick solution. So there's a mutual dependency."

Walter Laqueur, chairman of the International Research Council of the Center for Strategic and International Studies: "The media are a terrorist's best friend. . . . [Terrorists] are the superentertainers of our time."

Professor Raymond Tanter, political scientist at the University of Michigan: "Since the terror is aimed at the media and not at the victim, success is defined in terms of media coverage. And there is no way in the West that you could *not* have media coverage because you're dealing in a free society."

Thus, the terms of the debate are complex and the questions raised by television's relationship to international terrorism are far more numerous than the available answers. But the dilemma won't go away, and could get a lot worse. In a report prepared for the United States State Department, the Rand Corporation puts it this way: "It is hard not to conclude that terrorism judged on its own terms—as a way to get attention and arouse alarm—has been a success, and that highly visible success is likely to lead to further incidents of terrorism."

The Medium in the Middle

Terrorism of the Supermedia Age is less than ten years old [a CIA official told a reporter]. It begins with the death of Che Guevara and the victory of Israel in the Six-Day War. Rural guerrillas in Latin America and elsewhere, after failing to attract mass support, shifted their offensives from the countryside to the cities, where they would be within reach of big media.

At the same time, the Arab world realized that Israel could not be dislodged militarily, so certain activists among them took their cause to the urban centers of Europe and the Middle East. The Palestine Liberation Organization, don't forget, was not founded by rural peasants. Many PLOers had been educated in European universities and had absorbed techniques of civil protest and media manipulation.

By the late 1960s, terrorist acts were commonplace in the world's daily news diet. And a newly declassified CIA study predicts that terrorist acts in the United States, carried out by foreign-linked activists, will increase in the next few years.

The number and pattern of such acts have suggested to experts that terrorists learn, and are inspired by, the exploits of other terrorists; that media treatment of terrorist acts subtly fosters a global atmosphere in which further violence is probable and even predictable; and that the enormous publicity "payoff" of terrorism makes it irresistible to certain types of political zealots.

"The first several hijackings aroused the consciousness of the world to our cause and awakened the media and world opinion much more—and more effectively—than twenty years of pleading at the United Nations," says Zehdi Labib Terzi, the Palestine Liberation Organization's chief observer at the UN.

Surely, the PLO's success at dramatizing its grievances has been more spectacular than that of almost any other activist group—even though the PLO now claims to confine its hostilities to the "occupied territories" of Israel. "The media have not always been thorough in their presentation of PLO activities," Terzi complained recently. They often fail, he said, to provide sufficient background to let viewers perceive the terrorist act in its full context.

Violence by its nature is an integral part of any liberation movement, said Terzi, and is not always done merely for publicity. One of the PLO's problems, he insisted, is that TV and print newsmen too often and too easily ascribe terrorist acts to the PLO when in fact the acts were committed by free-lance pro-Palestinian desperadoes having no PLO connection. He is encouraged, he said, that networks and stations have recently begun telephoning him after bombings and hijackings to determine if the PLO was actually involved.

But the PLO is hoist upon its own media petard, having earned a worldwide reputation as a terrorist group. Says Robert Fearey, [former] special assistant to the Secretary of State and coordinator for combatting terrorism:

> Yasir Arafat [chairman of the PLO] is not now involved in international hijackings, murders and kidnappings because he found those tactics counterproductive to his political goals—causing more revulsion than positive gains. That earlier period put the PLO on the map. Later, when they began to aspire to government status, however, it became invidious for them to continue these horrible acts outside Israel, so they stopped them.

Thus, the media—which helped create the PLO—were instrumental in forcing a major shift in that group's global strategy.

Other terrorist groups, however, are still cavorting on the world stage, and TV news organizations are regularly faced with tough decisions about how to handle them. No serious critic says that censorship is the answer, or recommends any significant level of *self*-censorship. If TV withholds legitimate news of violent acts, rumor will take over (most experts say) and become a worse problem than the actuality. "The terrorists will have won," says a State Department official, "if we throttle our free press in the attempt to minimize terrorism. It would be like grounding all our commercial airliners to discourage potential hijackers."

Even if television did censor itself, clever activists would test the medium until they found the point where the self-censorship broke down. "They'd simply conduct extravaganzas that could *not* be ignored," speculates political scientist Raymond Tanter of the University of Michigan.

Similarly, as incidents of political terror proliferate, and as TV news editors as well as TV audiences become desensitized to the shock of such violence, terrorists will tend to up the ante to assure that their voices will be heard. Professor Irving Howe, a longtime student of political movements, puts it this way: "Terrorists are driven to greater, more extreme violence to force the press and the world to pay attention. There is a kind of tacit complicity between the sensationalism of the media and the sensationalism of the terrorists."

"Right to Know"—An Absolute?

A few theorists deny that terrorists would escalate their mayhem if TV played down political violence.

Ninety percent of these events are the homespun efforts of bumbling dum-dums trying to make names for themselves [says psychiatrist Dr. David Hubbard]. They wouldn't even *think* of bombing and hijacking, unless you guaranteed them a rostrum. So if the media cut their coverage down to the importance of other minor news, these men wouldn't act.

Hubbard disputes TV newsmen's contention that the public's right to know—as well as the journalist's right to report—is absolute. Is it the public's right to know or the economic interest of television that these men are concerned with, he wonders. TV news departments can hardly deny that sensational events draw viewers. But doesn't the medium have a responsibility to the public to study the consequences of its actions? he asks.

Despite the self-righteousness of many TV newsmen, Hubbard insists that terrorism is

reported by a controlled press—controlled by the unconscious career needs of its editors and correspondents, and by economics in the form of the Nielsen ratings. . . . We should assemble and petition redress of our grievances against media misuse of its legal right to report news.

TV news executives, naturally, are sure they're doing the very best they can with a problem that has no single solution. ABC News boss William Sheehan says: "I don't think it's our job to decide what people should not know. The news media are not the reason for terrorism even though they may sometimes become part of the story." Television's right to report is indeed absolute, says Sheehan, but TV newsmen must make their own judgments about when to exercise that right, and when to use restraint.

CBS News executive William Small's views are unequivocal:

It's always better to report than not to report [he insists]. We have policies that touch on terroristic acts, but obviously these are ad hoc decisions. If we thought at any time that life was endangered, or a terrorist act could happen as a direct result of our reporting, our policy permits us to delay the story. But that never happens.

The worst thing that could happen in this country—far worse than any act of terrorism—would be a loss of faith in the news reporting of television and newspapers. We're not educators, we're not sociologists. Our role remains that of reporter—to give people as much information as we can, as straight as possible and with as little hysteria as possible.

We don't want to be used or misused [Small added]. I don't believe in terrorist acts, but I do believe that people with grievances have a right to get their story told. We shouldn't be suppressing speech any more than we should allow others to suppress our reporting.

A Continuing Problem

The dozen or more experts consulted by *TV Guide* for this series are unanimous in believing that terrorism is not going to go away. Indeed, three European governments (France, West Germany and Great Britain) recently established an antiterrorist league to combat, jointly, expected *new* eruptions of violence. And secret reports compiled by intelligence agencies of the fifteen NATO countries indicate that a terrorist network of extremists from many nations—Basques, Bretons, Irish, Arabs, Japanese, Latin Americans and others—has its base in Paris and is financed by a handful of radical governments.

A CIA deputy director predicted recently that "terrorism will get worse" and may even involve the use of nuclear devices. Terrorists could steal enough nuclear materials to make their own bombs. "If this happens, they could hold a whole city hostage to achieve their goals," he said. "It would be the ultimate act of terrorism."

Thus the problem of how to respond to violent political action remains crucial. Solutions come in different shapes and sizes, not all of them promising. A few suggestions were proffered by the experts we consulted for these articles. They proposed, for example, that television news organizations (local and national, in the United States and abroad) should:

☐ minimize the "how-to" aspects of terrorist acts to prevent their being repeated by other terrorists who might learn specific details of how to plant bombs, hijack planes or abduct hostages

☐ downplay or even, in some cases, omit the names of terrorist groups that "claim credit" for violent acts, thereby denying them the expected publicity payoff while not denying viewers news of the crime itself

☐ 'imit *live* coverage of kidnappings, skyjackings and other crimes involving hostages. Since it does not serve the public's right to know in any substantive way, it should be curtailed voluntarily by TV people to avoid giving succor to the criminals and endangering the lives of the hostages while the event is still in progress.

☐ give proper emphasis to the inhuman and barbarous aspects of terrorist acts, and not only to their action-adventure aspects, which sometimes tend to appear glamorous when described by TV reporters

☐ refrain from routinely interviewing terrorist leaders on camera to avoid conferring upon them an unwarranted respectability

☐ give air time to terrorist acts only in realistic proportion to their objective news value, no matter how exciting the news film one happens to have on hand

☐ emphasize statistics that indicate the low likelihood of success for such crimes as abduction and hijacking, thereby discouraging would-be offenders

☐ provide documentaries and thoughtful analysis on the range of problems facing a community or a country, and even access to the airwaves for the voices of reason among dissident groups, thereby reducing the likelihood of their resorting to violence to have their grievances heard

Modern forms of terrorism caught everybody off guard [says the Rand Corporation's Brian Jenkins]. It's taking a while to figure out how they work and how to cope with them. And now people in the media, as well as in government, are reaching some conclusions. The kinds of questions that weren't being asked two or three years ago are now being asked. We're seeing a process of reflection and analysis.

JUSTIFIED OR NOT? A DEBATE [3]

Michael Walzer:

The November 22 [1975] issue of the *New Republic* carried two articles on terrorism, by Roger Morris and J. Bowyer Bell [See "Europe Under the Gun," by J. B. Bell, in Section II, above.] which in some measure responded to my piece, "The New Terrorists" (August 30, 1975). Morris and Bell reflect a widespread attitude (expressed also in many of the letters I have received) that seems to me more frightening than terrorism itself. It might best be described

[3] From "Terrorism: A Debate." *New Republic.* 173:12-15. D. 27, '75. Reprinted by permission. Michael Walzer, professor of government at Harvard, and Roger Morris, free lance writer, are contributing editors of the *New Republic.* Dr. J. Bowyer Bell is an academic expert on terrorism, author of the recently published *Terror Out of Zion,* presently associated with the Institute of War and Peace at Columbia University.

as a loss of moral confidence. In Morris' case, the loss is reflected as much in the style as in the substance of his essay.

He starts by accepting the distinction I suggested between "the calculated limited murder of political personalities that began in the nineteenth century" and contemporary terrorism with its random killing. Then he tries to explain the shift from the one to the other: "In some degree, at least, we may be watching a violent reaction to the failure of mass democracy no less rationalized than the attack on individuals in an age of aristocratic or colonial government." An enigmatic sentence: of course, terrorism is *rationalized* in terms of an antidemocratic ideology; every political view is rationalized in some terms or other. The queston that has to be faced takes a different form: *Is it rational?* Mr. Morris wants to suggest that it is, but he does not want to say so. And for good reason. He goes on: "For the revolutionaries of the 1970s, the perceived hypocrisy and betrayal of the American system might easily be seen as a common responsibility, every citizen an accomplice in the status quo . . ." Note again the indirect phrasing: *might easily be seen.* Squinting, one can see almost anything, but is it there? Does that common responsibility actually exist? Imagine that during the Vietnam war, American terrorists had placed bombs in restaurants and bars, bus stations, supermarkets and schools. Would the people they killed— all of them?—any of them—have been "responsible" for the war? Morris knows the answer, but he does not give it.

He also knows more than he says about the effectiveness of terrorism. We can't go on pretending, he argues, that terrorist violence is bound to be ineffective.

Vicious and wanton as it has been, PLO [Palestine Liberation Organization] terrorism is unquestionably a factor in the Middle East . . . Terror was an influence in Vietnam, both in the atrophy of the Saigon government and in provoking US escalations . . . It has altered the politics of Northern Ireland beyond return, and may lead there, for better or worse, to a partition that no other means could have produced.

Now, it's never been claimed that terrorism has no effects; dead bodies are its first and most lasting effects, but there are no doubt other effects as well. What we need to know is whether terrorism has or can have the effects the terrorists claim to be seeking, and whether it has or can have effects that liberals and Socialists might conceivably endorse. Let's look at Morris' cases. (I will leave aside the Vietnamese case, since he is presumably referring to the Vietcong assassination campaign of the early 1960s, which was aimed at government officials and—whatever one wants to say about it—was not an example of random killing.) The PLO claims to have as its goal the creation of a democratic secular state in which Jews and Arabs might live in peace. Clearly, however, the indiscriminate murder of Jews does not serve that end. What end does it serve? It might one day lead, along with many other factors, to the creation of a Palestinian state, but a state of a particular sort, one dominated by the terrorists. If one aimed at any other sort of Palestinian state, one might imagine other ways of getting it. Similarly with the "provisional" wing of the IRA [Irish Republican Army]: its stated end is a unified and democratic Ireland, and that is the one goal that its means will never produce. A new partition, perhaps; but then we would want to know—for better or for worse?

Does Terrorism Work?

Because he does not raise these questions, Morris manages to leave the reader with a vague sense that terrorism works. It may indeed work for the terrorists, but not for the rest of us. That has to be said, and firmly, or else the "repugnance" that Morris professes to feel and undoubtedly does feel in the face of terrorism will seem merely pious. One inevitably suspects that political acceptance hides just behind the outrage. I don't think it does, in this case; what is hidden is a great anxiety about expressing outrage.

The reasons for the anxiety are made clear in the last

paragraph of Mr. Bell's more extended and informative article. Bell is worrying about the possibility of a repressive response to terrorism:

Outraged indignation should fit uncomfortably on those who gave us the holocaust or the fire-bombing of Hamburg or a century of large-scale brutality, but it does not. More to the point, such indignation is partisan. The wave of protest over the Spanish executions indicates that some gunmen are more acceptable than others, especially if they have an odious enemy in a distant country . . . One man's terrorist is another's patriot. From the seat of power in Rome or London or Madrid the gunmen are wicked, evil men who must be destroyed by any means, by all means. And therein lies the danger.

This is an incredibly confused passage, but one that makes, again, a typical argument. Let's unravel it slowly, beginning with the Spanish executions. The executed men were accused of killing government officials, not of random murder. They had actually taken some care not to injure innocent bystanders, and one might therefore prefer them to, say, the IRA or the PLO without reference to the cause they served. In any case many of us who protested the executions did so because the so-called "terrorists" had not received anything resembling a fair trial—not because we believe that assassins, if their cause is just, can never be punished. We would protest executions of that sort wherever they took place. Finally the men and women who occupy "seats of power" in the democracies of Western Europe are not responsible for the holocaust or the fire-bombing of Hamburg. In what possible sense is it hypocritical for them to feel indignant if their countrymen are murdered? Bell's argument here is like the one we heard all through the Watergate crisis: everybody does it, why blame Nixon? Everybody does it, why be outraged at the IRA? In Watergate, the argument didn't work, since we all knew that Nixon was a "wicked man." But neither Morris nor Bell is willing to say the same about the "gunmen from the ditch."

And what about the rest of us? The implication of Bell's last paragraph, and of the way of thinking that I have taken him to represent, is that we should feel a kind of general guilt about state violence in the twentieth century and therefore hold back from attacking political terrorism. In fact, however, the same principles apply to the two sorts of brutality, and ought to be applied in every case. It is bizarre to suggest that because of the holocaust (or because of Hiroshima and Vietnam) the murder of innocent people in Belfast, London and Jerusalem should go uncondemned and unpunished. This is not moral delicacy; it is simply a failure of nerve.

J. Bowyer Bell:

First, one of the burdens of my article was that there is not nor is there likely to be a generally accepted definition of "terrorism" because even the killing of innocent people has been rationalized by states and revolutionaries on a variety of grounds. A great many who protested the Spanish executions, as Mr. Walzer is aware, were not unduly concerned about the slovenliness of Spanish judicial practice but rather about the nature of the government in Madrid. Many in Europe, indeed, are deeply sympathetic with the aims of the Basques and hardly outraged by their methods; what more effective means to oppose Spanish tyranny or establish a Basque republic might be suggested. In any case that the Basque gunmen are preferable because they are more discriminating than the PLO and more efficient than the Provisional IRA indicates a spectrum of indignation—and I did rather like "accused of killing government officials," a distinction undoubtedly lost on the widows of policemen shot down in ambush. However as long as Walzer intends to be outraged at every murder of innocent people —however defined—he is on sound logical and moral ground. The second point was that such indignation however logically and morally justified whether in Madrid or Jerusalem is not a sound foundation for an effective, ra-

tional response. Summary executions in Spain and bombing
raids on Palestinian refugee camps arising from such understandable indignation appear from a distance to be counterproductive.

Walzer, using the cases of the PLO and IRA, suggests
that it does not and cannot have the effect desired by
the terrorists. Both cases are moot, but the aspirations of
the Irgun Zvai Leumi and the Stern gang in the Palestine
Mandate and the IRA in Ireland were in part achieved by
quite familiar activities. There is now a twenty-six-county
Ireland and an Israel. Certainly revolutionaries in Aden
and Algeria and Angola feel that their armed struggles—the
imperialists' campaigns of terror—created facts, changed
history. Few would agree now (and none when they began)
that recourse to violence was unnecessary. There are those
who argue a terrorist act can be a means of saving life;
an assassin kills but one man—a Count Bernadotte—and
changes history. Even if he doesn't change history, still only
a single life has been lost, not a battalion. And often non-
violence engenders far more violence than the assassin. In
Northern Ireland in 1969, a civil rights demonstration began the slow but most assuredly not inevitable descent into
chaos. Anyway like most other acts of man, "terrorism"
works much as intended sometimes and sometimes it
doesn't. And, as Walzer notes, in every case the only certainty is dead bodies. As long as some few men see no
options but liberty or death, such bodies will be with us.
I would, for the rebels I support, opt for efficiency, dis-
crimination and rationality and, for the governments threatened by those I abhor, restraint, moderation and patience.
Thus, it is to be hoped, assuring fewer dead and greater
liberty.

Roger Morris:

Mr. Walzer is quite right that my description of terrorist
perceptions was carefully worded. I was trying for a moment
to draw beyond the usual self-protective smugness on this

subject, to show how the "rationality" of terrorism "might" look to its adherents. That Walzer saw in that fugitive effort some "moral" flaw (with "political acceptance" of murder lurking close in the margins) is an alarming illustration of the problems we face in coming to grips with the new terror.

The question of general and individual citizen responsibility for state policy in mass democracy is one of the most elusive in modern politics. Walzer's certainty about the "innocence" of random parts of the populace does not make the matter less arguable—nor, I'm afraid, does it save any of us from those who believe the opposite.

Would indiscriminate terrorism in the United States during the Vietnam war have struck at the "responsible," with any palpable effect therefore on the course of the war? We just cannot dismiss that question. As Nixon understood so well, the ground war had to end eventually because the draft of the middle class and the American coffins coming home were too close, too costly a price to pay. We went on with relative impunity, however, savaging a people with computers from thirty-five thousand feet, and we reelected by the greatest margin in history the man who ordered it. Did we continue that detached genocide because it cost *us* so little? Who *was* responsible? Nixon? Kissinger? The tens of thousands whose telegrams poured in to reinforce the worst instincts in an otherwise vacillating President after his speeches about "silent majorities" and "pitiful helpless giants"? Can we so easily believe that the carnage would not have ended years sooner had Americans suffered directly some bloody consequences of their growing indifference to the war after 1970? In these terms, are "responsibility" and the "rationality" of terror as simple as Walzer suggests?

And if Vietnam and our own psychology are too painful to look at as susceptible to terrorist retribution, are we similarly ready to banish this unwieldy problem of "common responsibility" from the millions who voted for and tolerated Hitler or who cooperated in Stalin's terror. Evil is indeed banal. But I suppose it depends on one's vantage point to see the ambiguity in which that leaves so much that Walzer seems to take for granted.

As for the effectiveness of terror, again I'm not so comfortably sure, as Walzer obviously wants to be, that it doesn't work. "Clearly," he says, the murder of Jews can't attain the PLO goal. Aside from the foolish presumption of being "clear" about any outcome in the Middle East, there's a lot of evidence, from the halls of the UN to the Israeli cabinet, that that's precisely what will happen. And the new Palestinian state will be defying every precedent of modern history (including Israel and the post-independence demise of the Irgun) if its governance doesn't very soon pass from the soldiers to the stolid bureaucrats waiting in Beirut and Amman.

Then there's Walzer's truncated Catholic Northern Ireland pointlessly cut adrift by the IRA bombers. Do we really believe that entity wouldn't be joined to the republic, with Whitehall's blessing as well as the good riddance of the Protestant successor state? Perhaps not. But that's easily as plausible as anything else, and that too would be a realization of terrorist goals. Let me correct here what Walzer deplores in my article as "a vague sense" that terrorism can be successful: I think we are tragically myopic if we deny for a moment that it does and will work.

"The Outrage That Leads to Terrorism"

But what about "the rest of us," Walzer asks with that same revealing phrase twice in a thousand words. The "rest of us" indeed. Though I don't know Walzer, I have a sinking suspicion that our disagreement here belongs too much to the sociology of knowledge. "It would not be difficult to imagine," he says for example, "other ways" than terrorism to realize a Palestinian state. The awful reality, of course, is that it has been not only difficult but impossible for many Palestinians in their wretched camps to "imagine" those "other ways," just as Walzer in his position finds it so impossible to entertain the conceivable rationality of terrorism. He worries about my anxiety to express outrage at terrorism; I wonder about his capacity to understand the outrage that leads to terrorism. I wonder too how durable his sure and detached moralism would remain after Israeli Phantoms napalmed *his* family, after the British army occupying Cambridge threw *him* in a concentration camp for breaking a curfew.

He reassures us that the "same principles" apply, or "ought" to apply, to state violence as to terrorism. But as Walzer the distinguished scholar knows very well, there is that fatal difference in reality between the "is" and the "ought." We hunt and judge and sometimes execute our terrorists. When does the trial begin for the Israeli pilots who killed seventy-four people the other day in Lebanon, the hundreds of American officials who planned and carried out a criminal war in Indochina, the surviving participants in the Hiroshima decision, the Bangladesh and Burundi genocide, the Chilean massacres? Surely we have the elemental honesty to admit to ourselves that morality, justice and retribution are still largely a matter of who's in the saddle. There is, to be sure, a difference between Nixon and the "gunman from the ditch": Nixon was pensioned off not for his complicity in incalculable human suffering, but only for the most flagrant flouting of the mores of the ruling elite.

As for a "loss of moral confidence," I should think that's the affliction of those who cannot confront terrorism in its own rationality, or honestly admit, as I suggested in my article, the similarities as well as the differences between terrorism and our own day-to-day lives. The last time I was accused of a "failure of nerve" was in an argument with a Pentagon general over the invasion of Cambodia. It's one thing for know-nothings to shun sensibility to oppression, to refuse to acknowledge that many people have no "other way," to flee from moral complexity and self-knowledge to some shrinking island of "outrage." When people of

Michael Walzer's gifts do it, we are in deeper trouble than I imagined.

Michael Walzer—Rebuttal:

The argument that I had to torture out of Roger Morris' first article he now makes openly and explicitly, and it is clear that I disagree far more with him than with Mr. Bell. This is what his position comes to: we are all participants in the crimes of Vietnam; we have no right, then, to condemn contemporary terrorism, but must seek instead to "understand" the desperation and outrage from which it springs. In the name of sensitivity, complexity and guilt—guilt above all, for this is a doctrine for masochists—we must accept terror as the legitimate weapon of the weak.

The major difficulty with this argument, aside from its sackcloth and ashes tone, is that terrorism, the random murder of innocent people, is a *new* weapon while outrage and desperation are very old. For many years, leftist and nationalist groups rejected terror, and even today the question whether or not to kill the innocent is an issue in every radical group (except in the PLO where, so far as the public record shows, no opposition to terror on a principled basis has ever arisen). The issue is angrily debated, on both moral and political grounds. Morris' position gives us no access to these debates. He is endlessly eager to understand the terrorists, but he does not even see their opponents. I don't mean the "ruling elites," but the men and women inside the Algerian FLN and the IRA and other similar groups who try to say no to murder. And he simply ignores the distinction that revolutionary militants once made between aiming at political targets and the deliberate premeditated killings of innocents.

There are two traditional leftist arguments against terrorism. The first is simple and direct: we don't kill innocent people; that's what *they* do, the forces of privilege and reaction; indeed, that's one of the ways we know who *they* are. The second argument is more political in character, though it also has moral implications: terrorism is not and cannot be a mass activity; it is the work of a small band of militants; inevitably it enhances the self-regard and power of an elite and undercuts the possibility of democratic government. The alternative path is mass organization, strikes, demonstrations, guerrilla war. These methods "work" when there is broad popular support, and don't work when there isn't—and surely that's what one wants to say of leftist politics generally, that it ought to succeed only insofar as it can mobilize masses of people.

Roger Morris is "sensitive" to oppression, but he has no interest in the politics of the oppressed. He is ready with an *a priori* endorsement of anything they do; he holds them to no standards, and that is finally to patronize them. They don't require that kind of understanding. They need to be supported when they act rightly, and to be criticized when they act wrongly—exactly as with the rest of us. It was indeed no loss of nerve to attack the Pentagon at the time of the Cambodian invasion; then Morris was insisting that there are moral limits on the use of power. But it is a loss of nerve to endorse terror: now Morris is refusing to apply those same limits, or for that matter any limits at all. To assuage his own guilt, he is willing to accept murder.

THE FUTILITY OF TERRORISM [4]

A few days before Christmas [1975] a group of terrorists broke into the OPEC [Organization of Petroleum Exporting Countries] building in Vienna; the rest of the story is still fresh in the memory and need not be retold. Coming so soon after the attacks of the South Moluccan separatists in the Netherlands [see "Incident in Holland," by William Mathewson, in Section II, above] the incident occasioned great hand-wringing and tooth-grinding among editorialists

[4] Article by Walter Laqueur, chairman of the Research Council of the Center for Strategic and International Studies, Washington, D.C. *Harper's Magazine*, 252:99-105. Mr. '76. Copyright © 1976 by *Harper's Magazine*. All rights reserved. Reprinted from the March 1976 issue by special permission.

all over the globe with dire comments about the power concentrated in the hands of a few determined individuals and
harrowing predictions as to what all this could mean for
the future. Because the significance of terrorism is not yet
widely understood, such a nine days' wonder could be regarded as an action of world-shaking political consequence.
Yet, when the shooting was over, when the terrorists had
vanished from the headlines and the small screen, it appeared that they were by no means nearer to their aims. It
was not even clear what they had wanted. Their operation
in Vienna had been meticulously prepared, but they seemed
to have only the haziest notion of what they intended to
achieve. They broadcast a document which, dealing with
an obscure subject and written in left-wing sectarian language, might just as well have been broadcast in Chinese as
far as the average Austrian listener was concerned.

The Vienna terrorists claimed to be acting on behalf of
the Palestinian revolution, but only some of them were
Arabs and it is not certain that there was a single Palestinian among them. Their leader was the notorious "Carlos"
[Ilitch Ramirez Sanchez], a Venezuelan trained in Moscow
and supported by Cuban intelligence in Paris—a branch of
the Soviet KGB [Russian Committee of State Security]. Yet
the operation, according to the Egyptian press, was paid for
by Colonel Qaddafi [Muammar el-Qaddafi, head of the Libyan government]. The working of modern transnational terrorism with its ties to Moscow and Havana, its connections
with Libya and Algeria, resemble those of a multinational
corporation; whenever multinational corporations sponsor
patriotic causes, the greatest of caution is called for.

Similar caution is required if one is to avoid exaggerating the importance of terrorism today. It is true that no
modern state can guarantee the life and safety of all of its
citizens all of the time, but it is not true that terrorists
somehow acquire "enormous power" (to quote our editorialists) if they kidnap a few dozen citizens, as in Holland,
or even a dozen oil ministers, as in Vienna. If a mass murder

had happened in Vienna on that Sunday before Christmas,
long obituaries of Sheik Yamani and his colleagues would
have been published—and within twenty-four hours, ambi-
tious and competent men in Tehran and Caracas, in Bagh-
dad and in Kuwait, would have replaced them. Terrorists
and newspapermen share the naive assumption that those
whose names make the headlines have power, that getting
one's name on the front page is a major political achievement. This assumption typifies the prevailing muddled
thinking on the subject of terrorism.

Focus on Urban Centers

In recent years urban terrorism has superseded guerrilla
warfare in various parts of the world. As decolonization
came to an end there was a general decline in guerrilla
activity. Furthermore, rural guerrillas learned by bitter
experience that the "encirclement of the city by the countryside" (the universal remedy advocated by the Chinese
ten years ago) was of doubtful value if four fifths (or more)
of the population are city dwellers, as happens to be the
case in most Western industrialized countries—and quite a
few Latin American countries too. With the transfer of
operations from the countryside to the cities, the age of the
"urban guerrilla" dawned. But the very term *urban guerrilla* is problematical. There have been revolutions, civil
wars, insurrections, and coups d'état in the cities, but hardly
ever guerrilla warfare. That occurs in towns only if public
order has completely collapsed, and if armed bands roam
freely. Such a state of affairs is rare, and it never lasts longer
than a few hours, at most a few days. Either the insurgents
overthrow the government in a frontal assault, or they are
defeated. The title *urban guerrilla* is in fact a public relations term for terrorism; terrorists usually dislike being
called terrorists, preferring the more romantic guerrilla
image.

There are basic differences between the rural guerrilla
and the urban terrorist: mobility and hiding are the essence

of guerrilla warfare, and this is impossible in towns. It is not true that the slums (and the rich quarters) of the big cities provide equally good sanctuaries. Rural guerrillas operate in large units and gradually transform themselves into battalions, regiments, and even divisions. They carry out political and social reforms in "liberated zones," openly propagandize, and build up their organizational network. In towns, where this cannot be done, urban terrorists operate in units of three, four, or five; the whole "movement" consists of a few hundred, often only a few dozen, members. This is the source of their operational strength and their political weakness. For while it is difficult to detect small groups, and while they can cause a great deal of damage, politically they are impotent. A year or two ago anxious newspapers readers in the Western world were led to believe that the German Baader-Meinhof group, the Japanese Red Army, the Symbionese Liberation Army, and the British Angry Brigade were mass movements that ought to be taken very seriously indeed. Their "communiqués" were published in the mass media; there were earnest sociological and psychological studies on the background of their members; their "ideology" was analyzed in tedious detail. Yet these were groups of between five and fifty members. Their only victories were in the area of publicity.

Terrorist Myths

The current terrorist epidemic has mystified a great many people, and various explanations have been offered—most of them quite wrong. Only a few will be mentioned here:

Political terror is a new and unprecedented phenomenon. It is as old as the hills, only the manifestations of terror have changed. The present epidemic is mild compared with previous outbreaks. There were more assassinations of leading statesmen in the 1890s in both America and Europe, when terrorism had more supporters, than at the present time. Nor is terrorist doctrine a novelty. In 1884 Johannes Most, a German Social Democrat turned anarchist, published in New York a manual, *Revolutionary (Urban) Warfare*, with the subtitle "A Handbook of Instruction Regarding the Use and Manufacture of Nytroglycerine, Dynamite, Guncotton, Fulminating Mercury, Bombs, Arson, Poisons, etc." Most pioneered the idea of the letter bomb and argued that the liquidation of "pigs" was not murder because murder was the willful killing of a human being, whereas policemen did not belong in this category.

It is sometimes argued that guerrilla and terrorist movements in past ages were sporadic and essentially apolitical. But this is not so; the Russian anarchists of the last century were as well organized as any contemporary movement, and their ideological and political sophistication was, if anything, higher. The same goes for the guerrilla wars of the nineteenth century. The guerrilla literature published in Europe in the 1830s and 1840s is truly modern in almost every respect. It refers to "bases," "liberated areas," "protracted war" as well as the gradual transformation of guerrilla units into a regular army. The basic ideas of Mao and Castro all appeared at least a hundred years ago.

Terrorism is left-wing and revolutionary in character. Terrorists do not believe in liberty or egality or fraternity. Historically, they are elitists, contemptuous of the masses, believing in the historical mission of a tiny minority. It was said about the Tupamaros that one had to be a Ph.D. to be a member. This was an exaggeration but not by very much. Their manifestos may be phrased in left-wing language, but previous generations of terrorists proclaimed Fascist ideas. Nineteenth century European partisans and guerrillas fighting Napoleon were certainly right-wing. The Spanish *guerrilleros* wanted to reintroduce the Inquisition, the Italian burned the houses of all citizens suspected of left-wing ideas. Closer to our own period, the IRA [Irish Republican Army] and the Macedonian IMRO at various times in their history had connections with fascism and communism. The ideology of terrorist movements such as the Stern gang and the Popular Front for the Liberation of Palestine encompasses elements of the extreme Left and Right. Slogans change with intellectual fashions and should not be taken too seriously. The real inspiration underlying terrorism is a free-floating activism that can with equal ease turn Right or Left. It is the action that counts.

Terrorism appears whenever people have genuine, legitimate grievances. Remove the grievance and terror will cease. The prescription seems plausible enough, but experience does not bear it out. On the level of abstract reasoning it is, of course, true that there would be no violence if no one had a grievance or felt frustration. But in practice there will always be disaffected, alienated, and highly aggressive people claiming that the present state of affairs is intolerable and that only violence will bring a change. Some of their causes may even be real and legitimate—but unfulfillable. This applies to the separatist demands of minorities, which, if acceded to, would result in the emergence of non-viable states and the crippling of society. It is always the fashion to blame the state or the "system" for every existing injustice. But some of the problems may simply be insoluble, at least in the short run. No state or social system can be better than the individuals constituting it.

It is ultimately the perception of grievance that matters, not the grievance itself. At one time a major grievance may be fatalistically accepted, whereas at another time (or elsewhere) a minor grievance may produce the most violent reaction. A comparison of terrorist activities over the last century shows, beyond any shadow of doubt, that violent protest movements do not appear where despotism is worst but, on the contrary, in permissive democratic societies or ineffective authoritarian regimes. There were no terrorist movements in Nazi Germany, nor in Fascist Italy, nor in any of the Communist countries. The Kurdish insurgents were defeated by the Iraqi government in early 1975 with the greatest of ease, whereas terrorism in Ulster continues for many years now and the end is not in sight. The Iraqis succeeded not because they satisfied the grievances of the Kurds but simply because they could not care less about public opinion abroad.

Terror is highly effective. Terror is noisy, it catches the headlines. Its melodrama inspires horror and fascination. But seen in historical perspective, it has hardly ever had a lasting effect. Guerrilla wars have been successful only against colonial rule, and the age of colonialism is over. Terrorism did have a limited effect at a time of general war, but only in one instance (Cuba) has a guerrilla movement prevailed in peacetime. But the constellation in Cuba was unique and, contrary to Castro's expectations, there were no repeat performances elsewhere in Latin America. The Vietnam war in its decisive phase was no longer guerrilla in character. There is no known case in modern history of a terrorist movement seizing political power, although terror has been used on the tactical level by radical political parties. Society will tolerate terrorism as long as it is no more than a nuisance. Once insecurity spreads and terror becomes a real danger, the authorities are no longer blamed for disregarding human rights in their struggle against it. On the contrary, the cry goes up for more repressive measures, irrespective of the price that has to be paid in human rights. The state is always so much stronger than the terrorists, whose only hope for success is to prevent the authorities from using their full powers. If the terrorist is the fish—folowing Mao Tse-tung's parable—the permissiveness and the inefficiency of liberal society is the water. As Regis Debray, apostle of the Latin American guerrillas, wrote about the Tupamaros: "By digging the grave of liberal Uruguay, they dug their own grave."

The importance of terrorism will grow enormously in the years to come as the destructive power of its weapons increases. This danger does indeed exist, with the increasing availability of missiles, nuclear material, and highly effective poisons. But it is part of a wider problem, that of individuals blackmailing society. To engage in nuclear ransom, a "terrorist movement" is not needed; a small group of madmen or criminals, or just one person, could be equally effective—perhaps even more so. The smaller the group, the more difficult it would be to identify and combat.

Political terrorists are more intelligent and less cruel than "ordinary" criminals. Most political terrorists in modern times have been of middle- or upper-class origin, and many of them have had a higher education. Nevertheless, they have rarely shown intelligence, let alone political sophistication. Larger issues and future perspectives are of little interest to them, and they are quite easily manipulated by foreign intelligence services. As for cruelty, the "ordinary" criminal, unlike the terrorist, does not believe in indiscriminate killing. He may torture a victim, but this will be the exception, not the rule, for he is motivated by material gain and not by fanaticism. The motivation of the political terrorist is altogether different. Since, in his eyes, everyone but himself is guilty, restraints do not exist.

Political terror therefore tends to be less humane than the variety practiced by "ordinary" criminals. The Palestinian terrorists have specialized in killing children, while the Provisional IRA has concentrated its attacks against Protestant workers, and this despite their professions of "proletarian internationalism." It is the terrorists' aim not just to kill their opponents but to spread confusion and fear. It is part of the terrorist indoctrination to kill the humanity of the terrorist—all this, of course, for a more humane and just world order.

Terrorists are poor, hungry, and desperate human beings. Terrorist groups without powerful protectors are indeed poor. But modern transnational terrorism is, more often than not, big business. According to a spokesman of the Palestine "Rejection Front" in an interview with the Madrid newspaper *Plataforma*, the income of the PLO is as great as that of certain Arab countries, such as Jordan, with payments by the oil countries on the order of $150 million to $200 million. Officials of the organizations are paid $5,000 a month and more, and everyone gets a car as a matter of course; they have acquired chalets and bank accounts in Switzerland. But the "Rejection Front," financed by Iraq, Libya, and Algeria is not kept on a starvation diet either. The Argentine ERP and the Montoneros have amassed many millions of dollars through bank robberies and extortion. Various Middle Eastern and East European governments give millions to terrorist movements from Ulster to the Philippines. This abundance of funds makes it possible to engage in all kinds of costly operations, to bribe officials, and to purchase sophisticated weapons. At the same time, the surfeit of money breeds corruption. The terrorists are no longer lean and hungry after prolonged exposure to life in Hilton hotels. They are still capable of carrying out gangster-style operations of short duration, but they become useless for long campaigns involving hardship and privation.

All this is not to say that political terror is always reprehensible or could never be effective. The assassination of Hitler or Stalin in the 1920s or 1930s would not only have changed the course of history, it would have saved the lives of millions of people. Terrorism is morally justified whenever there is no other remedy for an intolerable situation. Yet it seldom occurs, and virtually never succeeds, where tyranny is harshest.

The Terrorist's Friends

Events in recent years offer certain obvious lessons to terrorists. These lessons run against the terrorist grain, and have not yet been generally accepted. For example, terror is always far more popular against foreigners than against one's own countrymen. The only terrorists in our time who have had any success at all are those identifying themselves with a religious or national minority. It is sectarian-chauvinist support that counts, not drab, quasirevolutionary phraseology; Irish, Basques, Arabs, and the rest have found this out by trial and error. The media are a terrorist's best friend. The terrorist's act by itself is nothing. Publicity is all. Castro was the great master of the public-relations technique, from whom all terrorists should learn; with less than three hundred men he created the impression of having a force of overwhelming strength at his disposal. But the media are a fickle friend, constantly in need of diversity and new angles. Terrorists will always have to be innovative; they are the super-entertainers of our time. Seen in this light the abduction of the OPEC ministers rates high marks.

The timing of the operation is also of paramount importance, for if it clashes with other important events, such as a major sports event or a natural disaster, the impact will be greatly reduced. Whenever terrorists blackmail governments, it is of great importance to press realistic demands. Democratic authorities will instinctively give in to blackmail—but only up to a point. The demand for money or the release of a few terrorist prisoners is a realistic demand, but there are limits beyond which no government can go, as various terrorist groups have found out to their detriment.

Psychiatrists, social workers, and clergymen are the terrorist's next-best friends. They are eager to advise, to assuage, and to mediate, and their offer to help should always be accepted by the terrorist. These men and women of goodwill think they know more than others about the mysteries of the human soul and that they have the compassion required for understanding the feelings of "desperate men." But a detailed study of the human psyche is hardly needed to understand the terrorist phenomenon; its basic techniques have been known to every self-respecting gangster throughout history. It is the former terrorist, the renegade, who has traditionally been the terrorist's most dangerous opponent. Once again, the terrorist should never forget that he exists only because the authorities are prevented by public opinion at home and abroad from exercising their full power against him. If a terrorist wishes to survive, he should not create the impression that he could be a real menace, unless, of course, he has sanctuaries in a foreign country and strong support from a neighboring power. In this case political terrorism turns into surrogate warfare and changes its character, and then there is always the danger that it may lead to real, full-scale war.

Government Firmness Required

Recent terrorist experience offers some lessons to governments too. If governments did not give in to terrorist demands, there would be no terror, or it would be very much reduced in scale. The attitude of [Austrian] Chancellor Bruno Kreisky and his Minister of the Interior, who virtually shook the terrorists' hands, is not only aesthetically displeasing, it is also counterproductive. It may save a few human lives in the short run, but it is an invitation to further such acts and greater bloodshed. However, it would be unrealistic to expect determined action from democratic governments in present conditions. In wartime these governments will sacrifice whole armies without a moment's hesitation. In peace they will argue that one should not be generous with other people's lives. Western politicians and editorialists still proclaim that terrorism is condemned "by the whole civilized world," forgetting that the "civilized world" covers no more than about one fifth of the population of the globe. Many countries train, equip, and finance terrorists, and a few sympathetic governments will always provide sanctuary. Western security services may occasionally arrest and sentence foreign terrorists, but only with the greatest reluctance, for they know that sooner or later one of their aircraft will be hijacked or one of their politicians abducted. Ilitch Ramirez Sanchez ("Carlos"), the Venezuelan terrorist, is wanted in Britain for attempted murder, yet Scotland Yard decided last December not to press for his extradition from Algiers. For, in the words of the London *Daily Telegraph*, "the trial of an international terrorist could lead to political repercussions and acts of terrorist reprisals." A good case could be made for not arresting foreign terrorists in the first place but simply deporting them. The European governments on a West German initiative have had some urgent deliberations in recent weeks as to how to collaborate in combating terror. But, according to past experience, it is doubtful whether international cooperation will be of much help unless it is worldwide.

These observations do not, of course, refer to the South Moluccans, the Kurds, and other such groups in the world of terrorism. They fight only for national independence; they are on their own because they fulfill no useful political function as far as the Russians and the Cubans are concerned. The Libyans and Algerians will not support them because they belong to the wrong religion or ethnic group, and even South Yemen will not give them shelter. They are the proletariat of the terrorist world.

Terrorism is, of course, a danger, but magnifying its importance is even more dangerous. Modern society may be vulnerable to attack, but it is also exceedingly resilient. A plane is hijacked, but all others continue to fly. A bank is robbed, but the rest continue to function. All oil ministers are abducted, and yet not a single barrel of oil is lost.

Describing the military exploits of his Bedouin warriors, Lawrence of Arabia once noted that they were on the whole good soldiers, but for their unfortunate belief that a weapon was dangerous in proportion to the noise it created. Present-day attitudes towards terrorism in the Western world are strikingly similar. Terrorism creates tremendous noise. It will continue to cause destruction and the loss of human life. It will always attract much publicity but, politically, it tends to be ineffective. Compared with other dangers threatening mankind, it is almost irrelevant.

IV. EFFORTS TO COMBAT TERRORISM

EDITOR'S INTRODUCTION

According to estimates, there are at most some 5,000 terrorists loose in the world today. It is an indication of the concern they have aroused that in the normal course of everyday activities diplomats, business leaders, and all airline travelers are now subjected to costly and sometimes disruptive security precautions. In recent years, as accounts in this section show, governments have taken increasingly strict measures to combat terrorism. Yet, as a recent State Department release pointed out, at least four governments—those of Libya, South Yemen, Iraq, and Somalia—have at one time or another given encouragement to terrorist acts by providing funds, a place of refuge, or other aid and comfort. When governments fail to agree, of course, the preventive actions taken by some are accordingly weakened.

Israel and the United States have thus far led the field in taking a hard line on terrorist demands, but many governments in Western Europe appear to be learning the lesson that appeasement only encourages further outrages. Consequently they are moving toward a sterner position. The Council of Europe has adopted an agreement that would require the extradition of all terrorists to the country where the crime was committed. This convention is in the process of ratification by member governments.

The section opens with an article from *U.S. News & World Report* that details the problems involved in making airports more secure against random bombing and other forms of terrorism. This is followed by an address delivered before the International Committee of the Public Relations Society of America by Lewis Hoffacker, formerly special assistant to the United States Secretary of State, outlining

steps being taken by the United States government to combat terrorism. The third article, from *Aviation Week & Space
Technology*, provides evidence of similarly tough methods
being adopted by some of the Arab states of the Middle
East. Israel's antiterrorist policies are described in the next
article by Terence Smith of the New York *Times*, who
notes that few other governments have gone so far. The
section concludes with an article from *Aviation Week &
Space Technology* that reports on the extradition treaty
being enacted in Europe.

PROTECTING AIRPORTS FROM TERRORISTS [1]

Reprinted from U.S. News & World Report

The bombing of New York's La Guardia Airport [in
December 1975] has raised new concern about an old problem:

How can planes and airports be made secure against
terrorists?

Air officials were just beginning to feel confident about
solving one phase of the problem—hijacking of airliners. It
had been more than three years since a plane had been successfully hijacked in the United States.

Then on December 29, the La Guardia bomb exploded
in a holiday-season crowd, killing eleven people and injuring about seventy-five.

This pointed up a danger that present security measures—aimed at skyjackers—cannot control. And it set off a
flurry of official planning to plug the security gap.

President Ford, saying "we must do something in the
area of terrorist control," ordered a special task force set
up to recommend new measures. . . . [Representative John
Murphy, Democrat, New York] proposed legislation to require X-ray inspection of all baggage checked on airliners.
[The bill died in committee.—Ed.]

[1] From "Can Airports Be Safe from Terror Bombings?" *U.S. News & World
Report*. 80:58. Ja. 12, '76.

But investigation of the La Guardia bombing showed the difficulty of devising any sure prevention system.

The La Guardia bomb was planted in a baggage-claim area. Police believe it was in a public locker. It could have been put there, officials point out, without ever going through the only screening now in effect—that of luggage which is carried aboard a plane in the hands of passengers.

One Federal Aviation Administration official told *U.S. News & World Report:*

The only possible way to cope with bombings in a busy US airport would be to examine every piece of luggage that comes in—including the hold baggage handled by the airlines.

That could be done, but with some 15,000 scheduled flights every day, you can see what this would do to air travel as we know it today.

For example, airport inspectors might physically examine every piece of luggage—as El Al does today on its small, twice-a-day flights from New York to Tel Aviv. Or they could use trained dogs to sniff out explosives in piles of luggage, or X rays to reveal the outlines of possible explosive devices inside passenger luggage. These are procedures we use now only when there is some reason to suspect a bomb may be hidden in the baggage compartment or area.

The only procedure now used routinely to guard against bombs in cargo-hold luggage is to require that every passenger checking such luggage have a valid ticket for the flight on which the luggage is to go. The theory, officials explain, is that a passenger would not be likely to bomb the plane on which he was riding.

Even thorough inspection of all passenger baggage, however, would not protect against bombs planted in lockers by airport visitors who were not plane passengers. To meet this problem, the federal task force is considering such ideas as requiring locker keys to be dispensed at a central point, making random checks of lockers and increasing police patrol of public facilities in airports. Meanwhile, many airports have closed their luggage lockers to the public.

Without locker checks, no kind of inspection would have prevented the last previous airport bombings. One was in Los Angeles, on August 6, 1974, when a small suitcase was left in a public locker, not checked with any airline. It exploded by the use of a time device, killing three people and injuring thirty-five. The other was at Boston's Logan Airport in September 1974, which also occurred in the baggage-locker area.

What aviation officials fear now is that terrorist groups will home in on dramatic airport bombings of this kind as a new means of getting attention. One danger signal: Within a few days after the La Guardia disaster, dozens of bomb threats were received at airports all across the country. Many airports closed down to make quick searches, none of which found any bombs.

Growing Threat

Latest FBI figures indicate that bombing already is on the increase, in the United States as well as in terrorist hot spots abroad.

For the first ten months of 1975, the FBI reported, there were 1,743 bombing incidents in the United States and Puerto Rico, compared with 1,486 in a similar period in 1974. The number killed was 51, compared with 18 the previous year, and the number injured was 259, compared with 150 in 1974.

The bombing of New York's busy La Guardia Airport, ironically, occurred just at the end of the year—1975—that had racked up the best safety record for America's commercial airliners in the history of the jet age. With only two fatal jetliner accidents during the year, deaths totaled 123, compared with 467 the previous year and a high of 499 in 1960. It was the lowest number of fatalities in the air since 1957.

Inspections of air passengers and their hand luggage for weapons, now standard at all US airports, was credited with thwarting some twenty-five potential hijackings during 1975 and turning up thousands of lethal weapons.

But bombings present a tougher problem. A Nashville airport official asks: "How far can you go?" with preventive measures. In his judgment, "there is really no protection" that can be guaranteed to stop bombing.

Now federal officials are keeping their fingers crossed and hoping that the bombing of crowded US airports doesn't turn into a new terrorist fad that could be the hardest yet to combat.

AMERICAN POLICY AGAINST TERRORISM [2]

The world has lived with violence and terror since the beginning of time. But we now are experiencing new forms of international terrorism which have reached the point where innocent people anywhere can be victimized. Nothing has more dramatically underscored this fact than the cruel tragedies at the Munich Olympics of 1972, the virtual epidemic of kidnappings in Latin America, and the wanton murder of two of our diplomats and a Belgian official in the Sudan.

These and other incidents bear witness to the terrible potential of a disturbed or determined person or group to terrorize the international community. Moreover, this capability for traumatic disruption of society appears to expand with the increasing technological and economic complexity of our society and with the added incentive of wide and rapid publicity.

What is terrorism? Last summer a UN group failed to agree on a definition of the term and became diverted by an inconclusive discussion of the causes and motives of terrorists. Such disagreement, however, should not deter us from getting on with the business at hand, which we, for our working purposes, regard as defense against violent attacks,

[2] From "The U.S. Government Response to Terrorism," address by Lewis Hoffacker, former special assistant to the Secretary of State, delivered before the International Committee of the Public Relations Society of America, New York, January 7, 1974. *Vital Speeches of the Day.* 41:266-8. F. 15, '75. Reprinted by permission.

by politically or ideologically motivated parties, on innocent bystanders who fall under our protective responsibility. I am talking primarily of Americans abroad and foreign officials and their families in this country. At the same time, we follow terrorism throughout the world, even though our people may not be directly involved, since this is a global phenomenon requiring global attention.

The US government has responded forthrightly to this serious challenge in fulfillment of its traditional responsibilities to protect its citizens and its foreign guests. In September of 1972 President Nixon established a Cabinet Committee to Combat Terrorism to consider, in his words, "the most effective means to prevent terrorism here and abroad." The Secretary of State chairs this Committee, which includes also the Secretaries of the Treasury, Defense, and Transportation, the Attorney General, our Ambassador to the UN, the Director of the FBI, and the President's Assistant on National Security and Domestic Affairs. This body is directed to coordinate interagency activity for the prevention of terrorism and, should acts of terrorism occur, to devise procedures for reacting swiftly and effectively.

Under the Cabinet Committee, a Working Group composed of personally designated senior representatives of the members of the Cabinet Committee meets regularly. It is this group . . . which is in daily contact as issues arise and incidents occur. While we would prefer to be a policy planning body dealing in preventive measures, we are geared to respond to emergencies. Over the past year and a half this interagency group has dealt with a wide variety of matters and in my view has made us as a government more effective in responding to the continuing threat from a variety of organizations or individuals seeking to strike at us at home and abroad. This is not to say that we have solved all the problems facing us. But we are using government-wide resources to better advantage and have at least reduced the risk to our people and our foreign guests. We must face the reality that there is no such thing as 100 percent security. But we are doing our job if we reduce risks to a practical minimum.

I would like to make clear at the outset that individual departments and agencies continue to manage programs dealing with terrorism under their respective mandates. The important difference is that these efforts, which deserve commendation, are now fully coordinated and consequently are greater deterrents to potential terrorists.

Stricter Security Measures

Intelligence is one of our more valuable resources in this self-defense endeavor. All security agencies have improved the quality of their intelligence relating to terrorism, and the Working Group ensures that this product is fully shared and coordinated throughout the government.

Abroad, security at our embassies and consulates has been steadily improved. Last summer [1973] the President submitted to the Congress a request for $21 million for personnel and materials to better our overseas security and hopefully reduce the risk which our official personnel suffer throughout the world. These funds are now being disbursed, based on highest prority needs at our posts abroad.

We are mindful that our mandate also covers unofficial Americans. For example, we are pleased to advise American businessmen with overseas interests. Our embassies and consulates are in constant touch with American businesses abroad, especially in such places as Argentina where they are particularly vulnerable. We are prepared to share with them security techniques and experiences. Although we may not agree on tactics such as the advisability of paying ransom, it is important that we stick together in tight situations such as Buenos Aires, where terrorists have taken advantage of serious internal security deficiencies to kidnap businessmen for increasingly higher ransoms. We were, e.g., concerned with the Bank of America case in Beirut, where a representative of Douglas Aircraft was murdered by bank robbers posing unconvincingly as fedayeen [Arab commandos operating especially against Israel].

Visa, immigration, and customs procedures have been tightened. The regulation allowing a foreigner to transit the United States without a visa has been suspended except for passengers with immediate onward reservations to a point outside the United States. This suspension applies to every traveller on a non-discriminatory basis and closes a loophole through which 600,000 visitors per year formerly passed.

In several categories of visa applicants who have been particularly susceptible to terrorist penetration, deeper screening of applications has shown some useful results.

In the fall of 1972 Congress approved a public law aimed at increasing protection for foreign officials and their immediate families in this country through the creation of federal criminal offenses for various acts directed at them and at other official guests. Under this legislation the FBI has investigative jurisdiction concurrent with that already held by local law enforcement authorities. This expanded legal coverage of our foreign guests will hopefully add a further deterrent to those who might be tempted to molest them. There has been one conviction under this law, and several other cases are now before federal courts or are expected to be submitted soon.

For some time the Postal Service has alerted post offices and other likely targets of letter bomb activity. Many hundreds of such devices have been circulating internationally. Some have been intercepted in this country by alert customs and postal employees with one injury sustained by a postal clerk in the process. Unfortunately a letter bomb exploded in the British Embassy last September [1973], maiming a secretary and illustrating dramatically that international terrorists have probably penetrated our security screen.

Hijacking within the United States has fallen off significantly since the beginning of . . . [1973]. This happy trend is not just a stroke of luck. Aside from the rigorous airport security program now underway, a principal factor in this favorable evolution is the bilateral agreement with Cuba whereby hijackers are denied asylum in that country. [This agreement expired early in 1977.—Ed.] Other countries, with or without our encouragement, have taken similar steps to close their doors to individuals who look for refuge from prosecution after a hijacking. Let us recall, at the same time, that the domestic variety of hijacker in the United States is usually different from those who operate abroad, with special ruthlessness, under the control of terrorist organizations.

International Measures

The United States has been busy internationally. We have been in the forefront of those who have sought tightened international air security. We have pressed for three important multilateral conventions dealing with hijacking: the 1963 Tokyo Convention, which in effect requires countries to return a plane and passengers if it has been hijacked; the 1970 Hague Convention, which says that countries should either extradite or prosecute the skyjackers; and the 1971 Montreal Convention, requiring that any kind of sabotage of aviation such as blowing up planes on the ground be dealt with by prosecution or extradition of the offenders. We had modest expectations as we sent a delegation to two joint air security conferences in Rome . . . [in 1973] in the hope that the international community would advance a step forward in tightening controls on skyjackers and aerial saboteurs. Despite our disappointment over the meager results in Rome, we are confident that there remains a sufficient sense of international responsibility to make possible other steps to discourage those who would threaten international air travellers. For one thing, we are seeing a steady stream of accessions to the aforementioned conventions by countries representing all ideologies. This, in itself, should have a good, deterrent effect. [For later information see "What Washington Wants Done," by Monroe Leigh and "Will Bargaining Work" by Judith Miller, in Section V, below.—Ed.]

In INTERPOL [International Criminal Police Organization coordinating police activities of participating nations against international criminals], in the Organization of American States, and in other appropriate forums, we achieve what is feasible in the way of multilateral discouragement of the international terrorist. Simultaneously we maintain quiet liaison with individual governments which share our abhorrence of terrorism. We are pleased, e.g., to assist others when they suffer hijackings by providing communications and other services even though the affected plane may not be over or in our country.

At the UN in 1972 we sought to prohibit the export of violence to innocent persons who are many countries, sometimes continents, removed from the scene of a conflict. This approach became bogged down in debate over so-called justifiable, as opposed to illegal, violence. Accordingly, we narrowed our objectives to more specific categories of offenses which because of grave and inhuman effect on innocent individuals or because of their serious interference with the vital machinery of international life, should be condemned by states of every ideology and alignment. We therefore supported in the last [1973] General Assembly a convention for protection of diplomats. The Assembly agreed in December to this measure, which requires that persons who attack or kidnap diplomats or officials of foreign governments or international organizations be extradited or prosecuted.

If in spite of all our efforts, an act of terrorism should occur, we are prepared to deal with it swiftly and effectively. Within the State Department, task forces can be assembled on short notice to manage such critical events as the Southern Airways hijacking, the seizure of American diplomats in Haiti, the murder of two of our officers in the Sudan, the kidnapping of our Consul General in Guadalajara, the hijacking last summer [1973] of the Japanese airliner out of Amsterdam, the attack on emigrant Jews in Austria last fall, various incidents at Rome and Athens airports, and the recent terrorism in Karachi and

Singapore harbors and in Kuwait. Such task forces are composed of selected specialists who can call on the full resources of the US government to rescue, or at least to monitor, the beleaguered parties. The State Department Operations Center, which is the site of such task forces, is in instant contact with the White House, Pentagon, CIA, and other agencies concerned, as well as foreign governments and overseas posts. By swift and intelligent action in such circumstances, we hopefully can overcome the terrorists by one means or another.

No-Ransom Policy

Tactics vary in each crisis situation, but one consistent factor should be understood by all parties concerned: the US government will not pay ransom to kidnappers. We urge other governments and individuals to adopt the same position, to resist other forms of blackmail, and to apprehend the criminal attackers.

I hasten to underline the importance which we attach to human life. We do not glibly sacrifice hostages for the sake of this admittedly firm policy. We believe that firmness, if applied with the best diplomacy we can muster, can save lives in the long run and probably in the short run as well.

We have had more terrorist experiences than we had anticipated in the past five years, during which period twenty-five of our officials abroad, who normally enjoy diplomatic protection, were kidnapped. Fifteen of these kidnapping attempts succeeded with ten individuals murdered and twelve wounded. When we Foreign Service people elected to follow this career, we appreciated that there were risks different in type and intensity from those to which we are exposed in this country. Abroad we experience increased threats of subversion, kidnapping, blackmail, civil disturbances, and politically motivated violence, including assassination. In my twenty-three years' Foreign Service experience, mostly abroad in the Middle East and

Africa, I have not seen any of our people flinch in a dangerous situation. We have learned to take reasonable precautions. We do not want to live in fortresses or armed camps. We use ingenuity to reduce risks. Most importantly, we must remind the host government of its undoubted responsibility for protecting foreigners within its territory. I recall, e.g., when I was once put under house arrest by an angry Minister, I reminded him and his government that that government continued to be responsible for my personal security and would face dire consequences if anything happened to me. I am glad to report that my consular colleagues rallied round me and after a week I was able to resume my normal movements.

It would be unfair to assign labels to countries as to their hawklike or dovelike qualities in facing up to the terrorist challenge. Each country naturally performs in the light of its own interests. Some are more cautious than others to avoid provoking militants who engage in terrorism. Even countries friendly to us are selfish about their sovereign right to decide what is best in a terrorist confrontation; whether or not, e.g., to yield to demands for ransom, release of prisoners, etc. Moreover, we in the United States have not found ourselves in excruciating circumstances such as some countries like Haiti or Mexico have undergone with foreign diplomats held in their territory under terrorists' guns.

The US approach to counter-terrorism is based on the principle derived from our liberal heritage, as well as from the UN Declaration of Human Rights, which affirms that every human being has a right to life, liberty, and "security of person." Yet the violence of international terrorism violates that principle. The issue is not war. The issue is not the strivings of people to achieve self-determination and independence. Rather the issue is—and here I quote from former Secretary of State [William P.] Rogers before the UN General Assembly:

The issue is whether millions of air travelers can continue to fly in safety each year. It is whether a person who received a letter can open it without fear of being blown up. It is whether diplomats can safely carry out their duties. It is whether international meetings—like Olympic games—can proceed without the ever-present threat of violence. In short, the issue is whether the vulnerable lines of international communication—the airways and the mails, diplomatic discourse and international meetings—can continue, without disruption, to bring nations and peoples together. All who have a stake in this have a stake in decisive action to suppress these demented acts of terrorism. We are aware that, aside from the psychotic and the purely felonious, many criminal acts of terrorism derive from political origins. We all recognize these issues such as self-determination must continue to be addressed seriously by the international community. But political passion, however deeply held, cannot be justification for criminal violence against innocent persons.

"Be Cool and Tough"

The United States has attempted to show leadership in stimulating a global preoccupation with this apparently growing international threat. We have not achieved all that we have sought in international cooperation. Our multilateral, bilateral, and unilateral efforts must, however, continue because the outlook is not as promising as it might be. There seems to be increased collaboration among terrorist groups of different nationalities. Such groups seem to be moving farther and farther afield, including toward North America. There is moreover evidence of ample financial sources for some terrorist groups not only from ransoms collected but also from governments which, for one reason or another, are sympathetic toward certain terrorist groups. And, last but not least, there seems to be no shortage of politico-economic-social frustrations to spawn terrorists on all continents.

Accordingly, we must increase our vigilance, our expertise, and our determination in the face of what may be an expanding threat to our personnel and other interests abroad, as well as on the home front. In fact, this global epidemic still threatens the very fabric of international order.

We as a government must be cool and tough—and I might add, sensitive—in responding to these vicious attacks against our citizens and other interests. As we seek to defend ourselves against this viciousness, we are not unmindful of the motivation inspiring the frustrated political terrorist, who feels he has no other way to fulfill his particular mission in life. As ways are found to convince him to reason otherwise, he must be made to understand *now* that it is unprofitable for him to attack innocent bystanders. In the meantime also, we as a government have a continuing obligation to safeguard the most fundamental right of all—the right of life. There is no reason why protection of this right and of our citizens need necessarily conflict with other human rights such as self-determination and individual liberty.

OTHER GOVERNMENTS GET TOUGH [3]

For the second time in as many months, Libyan-aided hijackers have been thwarted by armed intervention of the countries against which the crime has been committed. Last week [August 1976] Egyptian commandos overpowered three Libyan-financed hijackers who had taken over an Egyptair Boeing 737 and 101 passengers and crew on a flight from Cairo to Luxor. The Egyptian commandos, whose tenacity and training were demonstrated in their daring helicopter-borne raids into Sinai and their last-ditch defensive battles on the west bank of Suez during the 1973 war, executed a precision, coordinated attack on the hijackers after the aircraft landed at Luxor that sent two of the trio to the hospital severely wounded and rescued the 101 French and Japanese tourist passengers and the Egyptian crew of the aircraft.

[3] From editorial "Progress Against Hijacking," by Robert Hotz, staff editor. *Aviation Week & Space Technology.* 105:9. Ag. 30, '76. Reprinted from the August 30, 1976, issue of *Aviation Week & Space Technology* by special permission. Copyrighted © 1976 by McGraw-Hill, Inc.

The Luxor operation was neither as complex nor bloody as the July 4 Israeli raid on Entebbe airport that freed 103 Jewish passengers and an Air France crew, but it was executed in the same spirit that refused to accede to the hijackers' blackmail and took armed action against them. There is no doubt that the Israeli example at Entebbe spurred the Egyptian commandos performance at Luxor. "If the Israelis can do it, we can do it," Brigadier General Nabil Shukri, Egyptian commando leader, told a press conference after the successful operation at Luxor.

With Egypt and Israel taking the same type of response against the Libyan-aided hijackers, it is now up to the rest of the world to adopt a similar stance and to take all appropriate measures against the Libyan government of Colonel Qaddafi, who is financing not only the aerial pirates but every type of murderous terrorism from Ireland to Japan. Colonel Qaddafi has been sponsoring aerial hijackings for many years, and his country has turned into the principal refuge for hijackers and their hostages. Libyan diplomatic pouches are smuggling terrorist-type arms into every trouble spot in the world, and the Libyan embassies and consulates serve as arms distribution centers. It is long past the time when Libya should be isolated from the rest of the world economically, diplomatically and socially.

Ironically, when only western airlines were the target of the Libyan-financed hijackers, the rest of the Arab world tended to take a tolerant view of the problem and even offered haven to the fleeing criminals. Cairo itself was both a destination and refuge for hijackers who had murdered passengers, pilots and security guards of western airlines.

More recently, Colonel Qaddafi has directed his terrorism at his Arab neighbors, and that has apparently erased their indifference. Libya has engineered a series of terrorist bombings in Egypt, supported a coup to overthrow the current government of the Sudan and now extended its aerial piracy to Egypt. All of this has stimulated a mutual assistance pact between Egypt, Sudan and Saudi Arabia against Libya, but no visible results have yet emanated from this alliance. Action is overdue.

On the global scale, the threat of aerial piracy has been on a steadily diminishing scale for the past three years. All of the activity that seemed so futile during its early stages has slowly borne fruit. Cuba has opted out as a hijackers' haven. Closing of the Cuban refuge added to extensive and expensive passenger screening by US airlines has virtually eliminated domestic hijacking. The circle of other international havens also has narrowed.

Europeans Tackling Problem

Libya remains almost alone as a safe house for the aerial pirates and other terrorists. European airlines, which were originally loath to invest in tight passenger-security screening equipment and procedures, joined the trend in turn as their particular airports turned into murder scenes. European airport security is still far from perfect, as the Athens A-300B takeover demonstrated, but at least they are working on the problem, and indifference is long gone.

What is needed now to reinforce the progress already achieved and speed an absolute end to aerial piracy and blackmail is some crisp, unequivocal action by the reigning international bodies to outlaw both the hijackers and those who provide them sanctuary. [See "Europe Adopts New Measures," below.] As a practical matter, air hijacking has been narrowed to an unholy alliance between the radical elements of the Palestinian Arabs and the current ruler of Libya. That should be a thoroughly manageable problem if the more moderate elements of the Arab world join with Christians and Jews for combined action against the last hornet's nest.

However, unless such international bodies as the United Nations and the International Civil Aviation Organization reinforce world opinion with a flat condemnation of the

crime of aerial piracy, no matter in whose name or for
what cause it is committed, there is an opportunity for
this criminal technique to slither back into semi-respect-
ability when a new and temporarily plausible excuse for it
is forthcoming. The Afro-Arab bloc in these bodies has
been the stumbling block to a clear anti-hijacking policy
and the threat of sanctions against sanctuaries. But the
recent disgusting performances of [President] Idi Amin in
Uganda and Colonel Qaddafi in Libya make it clear it is
not a matter of race or religion but humanity itself that
is at stake.

ISRAEL TAKES A HARD LINE [4]

It is always an agonizing choice: the lives of the hostages versus the demands of the hijackers. If a government
gives in to save lives, will the action not ultimately cost
lives? Do justice and morality have anything to do with
it? In fact, does a government have the right to decide?
For Israel, which has coped with more than its share of
hijackings, these are questions of urgent concern.

The hijacking of an Air France plane and its diversion
to Uganda raised the questions all over again. The large
number of hostages involved, the remote location, the involvement of several sovereign states, the dubious attitude
of the Ugandan government, the uncompromising demands of the hijackers—all these made the episode especially difficult. It was a classic case study of the politics
of hijacking, in which Israel came to the brink of sacri-
ficing its basic policy of nonnegotiation with terrorists. At
the outset, it looked as though there was no choice but
to give in and release the imprisoned Arab guerrillas as
the hijackers were demanding from Israel and four other
states.

[4] From "With Life at Stake, How Can Terrorists Be Dealt With?" by
Terence Smith, staff correspondent based in Israel. New York *Times*. p E1. Jl. 11,
'76. © 1976 by The New York Times Company. Reprinted by permission.

Israel's policy of nonnegotiation has never been rigid. In 1968 Israel exchanged a group of imprisoned Arab guerrillas for the passengers and crew of an El Al plane; in 1969 two captured Syrian pilots were exchanged for two Israeli hijack victims jailed in Syria. There have been other, unpublished, instances when Israel negotiated with hijackers.

Since 1969, however, the government has avoided dealing openly with terrorists whenever possible. If there was an opportunity to fight back, it was exploited. On May 9, 1972, hijackers took over a Sabena airliner en route from Brussels to Israel. When the plane was on Israeli soil, a specially-trained Israeli commando unit broke into the cabin and shot it out, killing the two hijackers and one passenger in the process.

The combination of aggressive tactics and tight security has rendered El Al largely immune from hijacking. But the phenomenon has continued to grow on other airlines less careful about security. A total of 29 hijackings have been staged by Palestinian and pro-Palestinian groups since 1968, plus 3 airport massacres. Only 11 hijacking attempts have been foiled. The human cost has been heavy: 201 have been killed, 213 injured.

Softer Line in Europe

In contrast to Israel's hardline policy, most European countries elected to capitulate to hijackers. The governments of Greece, Austria, West Germany, France and Britain have released hijackers and their colleagues at one time or another. Huge cash payments have also been made, such as in February 1972, when Lufthansa paid $5 million to the Popular Front for the Liberation of Palestine to ransom a hijacked plane and its passengers. In every case, the motive has been to save innocent lives. But rarely has capitulation brought relief. On the contrary, one successful hijacking seems to encourage others, often on the same airline.

The Air France hijacking was unusually difficult for Israel because of the involvement of four other governments. In effect the government was proceeding on dual tracks simultaneously: It would negotiate if necessary, fight back if possible.

Are there other options? Are there alternatives that would avoid the terrible choice of risking the lives of innocent people?

Other suggestions have surfaced . . . [in Israel], but they are far from satisfactory. One proposal put forward was that Israel should employ counter-terror and threaten to execute one jailed guerrilla for every hostage killed in a hijacking. The idea has never been seriously considered.

Another suggestion was to reintroduce the death penalty for terrorism that causes loss of life. Capital punishment exists on the books in Israel but it is not implemented. Executing terrorists, some Israelis argue, would eliminate them as prizes for future hijackings. But that alternative could well lead to a retaliatory situation in which hijackers capture victims simply to execute them and even the score.

The only answer, it seems, is a coordinated, international effort to tighten airline security and prevent would-be hijackers from reaching the planes. Israel has called for such a campaign, although officials were skeptical that even the Uganda incident would bring about the necessary change in attitude.

Ironically, just four days before the Air France airbus was hijacked, the nine countries of the European Common Market reached agreement in Luxembourg on ways to increase security and combat international terrorism. [See "Europe Adopts New Measures," below.] A communiqué called for tighter coordination among the nine and an exchange of security personnel to study organization and tactics. Without Entebbe, it probably would have produced no more substantial results than the many similar communiqués that have preceded it. But perhaps the Air

France hijacking will provide the extra incentive necessary to bring about a fundamental change in the pragmatic politics of hijacking.

EUROPE ADOPTS NEW MEASURES [5]

Anti-terrorism convention that would make aerial hijackers and perpetrators of other terrorist acts liable for extradition to the country in which they committed the acts, no matter what the motivation, has been adopted by the nineteen-nation Council of Europe.

The convention, which has been approved unanimously by national delegates to the Council but must still be ratified by the individual member nations, is aimed at eliminating the loophole provided by so-called political crimes in avoiding extradition. Terrorist acts in which political motivation is a factor often fall outside the bounds of existing extradition treaties.

Where aerial hijacking is concerned, the convention goes a step further than earlier agreements such as the Hague Convention and the Montreal Convention because it makes extradition almost mandatory. The Hague Convention, for example, left to the discretion of individual signatory states the decision to either extradite or punish hijackers. [For further information on these conventions see "American Policy Against Terrorism," by Lewis Hoffacker, in Section III, above.—Ed.]

The convention adopted by the Council of Europe will be applicable only among those European nations that ratify the document. Only Ireland abstained from voting on the matter within the Council, and Council officials are thus optimistic that most members will ratify it.

The main goal of the convention will be to eliminate the judicial obstacle of political motivation in taking cus-

[5] From "Hijacker, Terrorist Extradition Sought by Council of Europe," *Aviation Week & Space Technology.* 105:23. N. 22, '76. Reprinted from the November 22, 1976 issue of *Aviation Week & Space Technology* by special permission. Copyrighted © 1976 by McGraw-Hill, Inc.

tody of and punishing terrorists. Among other infractions, the convention identifies aerial piracy, the taking of
hostages, kidnapping, sequestration, and the use of bombs,
grenades and firearms as terrorist acts, and it declares that
these actions "will no longer be considered as political infractions or as infractions inspired by political motives."

Strongest opposition to the convention has come from
France and from the Nordic countries, primarily on the
grounds that it threatens basic human rights. One of these
is the right to asylum. Nordic countries are opposed to
extradition of non-nationals who have been domiciled on
their territory. Council of Europe officials told *Aviation
Week & Space Technology* . . . , however, that the Nordic
countries are not opposed uncompromisingly to extradition, but rather are seeking to assure themselves a reasonable amount of time to review individual cases involving
requests for extradition.

Despite its opposition, France has indicated that it will
ratify the convention. . . . The French capitulation re-
flects the inclusion of certain escape clauses that potentially
could weaken the convention, or at least those aspects of
it concerned with extradition.

Article 13, one of the main escape clauses, notes that
any nation can, at the moment of signature of the convention, declare that it reserves to itself the right to refuse
extradition for any of the several infractions specified in
the convention if it considers them to be motivated politically.

More specifically, Article 3 of the convention provides
that a signatory can be exempted from the obligation to
extradite when there is serious reason to believe that the
request for extradition is itself motivated by "considera-
tions of race, religion, nationality . . . or political opinion."

To counterbalance these clauses, the convention stipu-
lates alternatively that where extradition is refused, the
nation in which the terrorists are being held will be
obliged to bring them to trial "without exception and

without undue delay." The primary emphasis, however, is on extradition.

At least three nations must ratify the convention before it becomes effective, and then it will be applicable only in and among those countries that have signed. It will not be effective between those European nations that have ratified it and nations outside Europe, as for example, in the case of the four Americans currently being held in France for the hijacking of a Delta Air Lines McDonnell Douglas DC-8 in 1972.

V. WHAT MORE CAN BE DONE?

EDITOR'S INTRODUCTION

If governments could agree, international efforts to stamp out political terrorism might succeed. A simple extradition treaty that would return terrorists to the scene of their crime would suffice. The problem is, of course, that the cure can in some cases be worse than the disease.

Such delicate questions have thus far stalled concerted international action against terrorism through the United Nations, as the first article in this section points out. The author concludes that the UN is not wholly to blame. In the second article a legal adviser to the United States Department of State sets forth the measures that Washington would like to see the international community adopt through the UN, including extradition arrangements. Next, journalist Judith Miller, writing in the New York *Times Magazine,* analyzes in detail current methods employed to deal with terrorist situations, challenging some long-standing policies of the United States and emphasizing that a "no-concessions" policy can sometimes prove counterproductive.

And, finally, Irving Louis Horowitz, professor of sociology and political science at Rutgers University, urges caution in the enactment of measures to combat terrorism. To stay free, he maintains, democratic societies must be willing to live with risks.

CAN THE UN ACT? [1]

"Had a Jewish state existed in the 1930s, we might well have decided, with the rise of Nazism, to endeavor to un-

[1] From "Hostages, Hijacking and the Security Council," by Homer A. Jack, secretary general of the World Conference on Religion and Peace. *America.* 135:94-7. S. 4, '76. Reprinted with permission of *America.* All rights reserved. © 1976 by America Press, 106 W. 56th St., New York 10019.

dertake an operation to rescue the inmates of the concentration camps." So spoke Israeli Ambassador Chaim Herzog during the UN Security Council debate in mid-July on the audacious Israeli rescue of hostages in Uganda. Challenging those nations that called the Israeli action a violation of Uganda's sovereignty, Mr. Herzog asked: "What would have been more important: Hitler's sovereignty or rescuing innocent people from a holocaust?"

The Security Council debate was at times fascinating, always political and occasionally tragic. The imaginative action of Israel in rescuing its hostages did not result in a corresponding action by the UN to rescue the world from further international terrorism. Only a deaf optimist at the UN could conclude that the rescue at Entebbe would result in new international action to lessen terrorism. On the other hand, only a cynical pessimist would assert that the problem is beyond human control.

World public opinion was outraged because of the killings at the Olympic Games in Munich in 1972. UN Secretary General Kurt Waldheim courageously put the item on the agenda of the 27th session of the General Assembly in September 1972. Despite his initiative, there was difficulty even maintaining the item on the agenda. Almost immediately, the political line-up became clear: the West and a few other states vs. the Arab bloc, the latter supported by much of the Third World and all of the Second, or Socialist, World. Since the Arabs still could not, at the time, immediately defeat the item, they were able to broaden it to include the causes of terrorism. The final title became something of a UN record for length: "Measures to prevent international terrorism which endangers or takes innocent human lives or jeopardizes fundamental freedoms, and study of the underlying causes of those forms of terrorism and acts of violence which lie in misery, frustration, grievance and despair and which cause some people to sacrifice human lives, including their own, in an attempt to effect radical changes."

The actual debate in the Sixth or Legal Committee in 1972 only accentuated the deep split among the UN members. The Western states wanted the UN to condemn terrorism strongly, to urge states to sign and ratify the existing instruments (the Tokyo, Hague and Montreal conventions [see "American Policy Against Terrorism," by Lewis Hoffacker, in Section III, above]) and to draft urgently needed new conventions. The Arab states emphasized state terrorism or acts of violence committed by states or toward states. They declared that state terrorism was worse than private terrorism because all the machinery and weapons of a modern state could be used. They suggested that more lives have been lost by state terrorism than individual terrorism. They insisted that, only after a study of causes, could measures be discussed and enacted.

An Ad Hoc Committee on International Terrorism, composed of thirty-five states appointed by the president of the General Assembly, later met in the summer of 1973. Subcommittees were organized to define international terrorism, to study the underlying causes and to consider measures to bring an end to terrorism. After much negotiation, a compromise report was almost approved, but at the last minute Algeria insisted on adding a qualifying sentence that, in effect, encouraged and defended the Palestinians and other terrorists. This was completely unacceptable to the Western members of the ad hoc committee. The chairman simply adjourned the committee without any conclusions to report to the General Assembly.

In the meantime, international terrorism accelerated. The United States State Department alone has spent more than $100 million to protect its personnel abroad from terror. In 1969, there were four major attacks against US ambassadors; in 1975, there were 19. Some studies show that an international terrorist involved in one of the kidnapping incidents in the past eight years had an 80 percent chance of escaping death or imprisonment. Indeed, the average sentence for the few who came to trial was only eighteen months. Of the 267 international terrorists apprehended since 1970, less than one half were still in jail as of September 1975.

Defining Terrorism

When the UN reaches a stalemate, or worse, because of the politicization of issues, an attempt is sometimes made—informally—to pass the issue on to a less political body. Thus, the UN Committee on Crime Prevention and Control presented the issue of terrorism to the Fifth UN Congress on the Prevention of Crime and the Treatment of Offenders which met at Geneva during September 1975. Participants in the congress—including judges, prosecutors and lawyers—also had difficulty in defining terrorism, calling it a "journalistic, emotive term," with no definitive legal status. The participants divided on whether acts of legitimate resistance against occupation could be regarded as terrorism. There was agreement that the forces of criminal justice against some forms of terrorism could be strengthened (1) by extending universal jurisdiction to such crimes (as is already the case for air piracy); (2) by strengthening the observance of extradition laws; and (3) by strengthening the cooperation of the International Criminal Police Organization (INTERPOL). It was suggested also that the UN arrange for a commentary on all relevant international conventions so that nations could fully understand them and have their legal validity clarified.

The final summary paragraph of the congress on this issue shows how this relatively depoliticized body also became immobilized in dealing with the problem:

In summary, participants were agreed that strong multilateral action was urgently needed to fight not only current levels of personally motivated transnational crime, especially violent crime, but also anticipated increases, and that clear-cut definitions of the difficult terms and concepts involved were necessary in order to permit both personal and political acts of terror-violence to be appropriately and differentially handled, whether

committed by individuals or by states. It was significant that
the congress did not approve of "political terrorism" while con-
demning other forms of terrorism. . . . But there was also agreement that politically inspired violence, committed for the sake
of gaining national independence or ethnic recognition or security, could not be expected to recede until the underlying
causes had been satisfactorily dealt with.

The Security Council Debate

On the day that Israel rescued the hostages at Entebbe,
the heads of state of the Organization of African Unity
(OAU) were meeting in Mauritius. Its new chairman, the
Prime Minister of Mauritius, Sir Seewoosagur Ramgoo-
lam, received information from his predecessor—President
Idi Amin of Uganda—of the "invasion of Uganda by Israeli commandos." The OAU voted to request an immediate meeting of the UN Security Council "to consider
this wanton act of aggression." Back in New York, the
council's fifteen members, under the chairmanship (for
July) of Italian Ambassador Piero Vinci, received the OAU
letter (and also communications from Mauritania, Israel
and Uganda) and discussed privately the frame of reference for the discussion.

The Africans insisted on restricting the agenda item
to the action of Israel at Entebbe. The Western members
wanted to broaden the item to include the hijacking of
the Air France plane and then the whole issue of terrorism. However, the West could not find the nine votes
necessary to put the broadened item on the agenda. They
did, however, prevent a prejudgment of Israel's action in
the title of the agenda item by putting the allegations of
the Prime Minister of Mauritius at least in quotation
marks: Complaint by the Prime Minister of Mauritius,
current chairman of the Organization of African Unity,
of the "act of aggression" by Israel against the Republic
of Uganda. Also, council members could, by tradition, discuss the widest parameters of any agenda item, including
submitting any draft resolution they wished.

Participating in the five meetings of the Security Council were, in addition to its fifteen members, Israel, Mauritius and Uganda, which were given seats at the council table. A number of other states also petitioned to speak. The debate that followed can be divided into a discussion of the rescue, interspersed with vituperation (for consumption back home or for bloc solidarity), the legal arguments and jockeying for passage of a resolution.

Three members of the Security Council that held swing votes were listened to carefully: Sweden, Panama and Rumania. Sweden, which had recently broken with the West on votes relating to the Middle East, in this instance said that, "while unable to reconcile the Israeli action with the strict rules of the Charter, [it] did not find it possible to join in a condemnation in this case." Rumania, the only Eastern European country maintaining diplomatic relations with Israel, asserted that "acts of terrorism against innocent persons cannot be considered as revolutionary means of struggle, even if they are undertaken in the name of a noble cause." Moreover, Rumania insisted: "We should not confuse or identify the struggle of national liberation of the peoples with terrorism." Panama asserted that the council must necessarily confront two acts of violence: "one perpetrated by an extremist group of Palestinian Arabs and Europeans," and "the other consummated by forces of the Israeli army." Panama concluded that "the question cannot be resolved by pronouncing a condemnation, whether directed against Israel or against those responsible for the hijacking."

The Palestinian Liberation Organization (PLO), unlike at earlier Security Council sessions this year [1976] on the Middle East, kept its distance from the council table as much as possible. The Popular Front for the Liberation of Palestine, which took responsibility for the hijacking, Israel called "one of the several terrorist groups joined together to form the PLO." . . .

The Security Council debate demonstrated the unique

character of the OAU, both in its role among the African states and between the latter and the rest of the world. No other continent, not even Latin America, possesses such an organization. Its forty-eight member states—every nation on the continent except Rhodesia, South Africa and Namibia (South West Africa)—maintain an unbelievable brotherhood despite the underlying divisions of tribe and nation.

The African states repeatedly asserted that Israel picked on Uganda because it was a small African country. Israel replied that the larger countries would never have sheltered the hijackers. Yet, the feeling of the Africans that their states made an easy target persisted and several spoke about the precedent being "extremely dangerous," especially for small states. Sweden observed that "any formal exceptions permitting the use of force or of military intervention in order to achieve certain aims, however laudable, would be bound to be abused, especially by the big and strong, and to pose a threat, especially to the small and weak."

The Legal Problems

Intertwined in the debate was a discussion of the legality of Israel's rescue of the hostages. The African states, and their supporters, cited the prohibition in the UN Charter against the "use of force against the territorial integrity or political independence of any state." Israel admittedly did use force against the territorial integrity of Uganda. Also cited was the new (1974) UN definition of aggression as the "use of armed force by a state against the sovereignty, territorial integrity or political independence of another state." This definition further warns that "no consideration of whatever nature, whether political, economic, military or otherwise, may serve as a justification for aggression." Many states indicted Israel before the Security Council as an aggressor, using a variety of strong adjectives.

Israel and its friends quoted additional law, both cases and textbooks, indicating that states have, on occasion, intervened to protect their nationals. This is the old Roman legal principle concerning the duty of a state to defend its nationals abroad. [D. W.] Bowett, in *Self-Defense in International Law* [Praeger, 1958], asserts: "The right of the state to intervene by the use of threat or force for the protection of its nationals suffering injuries within the territory of another state is generally admitted." [D. P.] O'Connell, in *International Law* [2d ed. Stevens, 1970] admitted that "traditional international law has not prohibited states from protecting their nationals whose lives or property are imperiled by political conditions in another state, provided the degree of physical presence employed in their protection is proportional to the situation."

Ambassador Salim Ahmed Salim of Tanzania indicated, however, that "the advent of the law of the Charter did away with all the traditional methods for a state to obtain satisfaction on a unilateral basis by employing measures short of war which were being resorted to in the past." He quoted [Georg] Schwarzenberger's volume, *International Law* [Praeger, 1971]: "Within the international quasi-order of the UN, the threat or use of force by individual member states against one another and against another non-member state is illegal, unless justified on the grounds of individual self-defense under Article 51 of the Charter." This is the position generally held by the African states and their supporters.

Israel's supporters, on the other hand, drew opposite legal conclusions. While admitting that Israel's action "necessarily involved a temporary breach of the territorial integrity of Uganda," US Ambassador [William W.] Scranton added that "there is a well-established right to use limited force for the protection of one's own nationals from an imminent threat of injury or death in a situation where the state in whose territory they are located is either unwilling or unable to protect them."

Two Unadopted Resolutions

Except for the disappointment experienced by all sides, the tangible outcome of the Security Council debate was nil. Of the two resolutions submitted, one was withdrawn and the other was defeated.

The three African members of the Security Council (Benin, the Libyan Arab Republic and the United Republic of Tanzania) submitted a resolution that would have had the Security Council condemn "Israel's flagrant violation of Uganda's sovereignty and territorial integrity" and demand that Israel "meet the just claims of the Government of Uganda for full compensation for the damage and destruction inflicted on Uganda." At the last meeting, the Africans did not press the resolution to a vote, for they did not have the required nine affirmative votes for passage. They could not persuade Panama or Rumania to vote with them. Even if they did, one of the three permanent members from the West—certainly the United States —would have cast a veto.

The United Kingdom and the United States also submitted a resolution. This reminded all states signatory to the Hague and Montreal conventions of the obligations flowing from their accession to these agreements. [See "American Policy Against Terrorism," by Lewis Hoffacker, in Section III, above.] Then the draft condemned "hijacking and all other acts which threaten the lives of passengers and crews and the safety of international civil aviation and calls upon all states to take every necessary measure to prevent and punish all such terrorist acts." The resolution also deplored "the tragic loss of human life which has resulted from the hijacking of the French aircraft" and reaffirmed "the need to respect the sovereignty and territorial integrity of all states in accordance with the Charter of the UN and international law." It finally enjoined "the international community to give the highest priority to the consideration of further means of assuring the safety and reliability of international civil aviation."

Six member states voted in favor of this Western resolution—France, Italy, Japan, Sweden, the United Kingdom and the United States. None voted against, and Panama and Rumania abstained. Taking a leaf from the common Chinese practice of not participating in a UN vote, the seven remaining member states announced their nonparticipation: Benin, China, Guyana, the Libyan Arab Republic, Pakistan, the USSR and the United Republic of Tanzania. Failing to receive the required majority of nine votes, the Western resolution was defeated. (If it had received nine votes, it still could have been vetoed by China or the USSR.)

Next Steps

The Security Council debate raised more questions about international terrorism than it answered. Those who thought that it might bring the world community out of the prolonged stalemate on this issue saw only meager indications of new progress. The action of Israel at Entebbe had such positive effect on Western public opinion that it did force all Western states to renew their previous solidarity on Middle East strategy. The action of Israel, especially since it was toward Uganda, may have pleased some African states privately, but their solidarity prevented it from surfacing. There is little indication, however, that the Third World is now prepared seriously to find new means of dealing with terrorism. Yet, slowly, new measures might evolve. The Soviet Union, for example, while standing solidly with the Third World, said it was "ready, along with other states, to take new additional measures against acts of international terrorism." No immediate action is expected, although the issue is bound to be discussed in the general debate and in the Sixth Committee of the 31st General Assembly convening late in September [1976].

In some circles, the UN's reputation is increasingly tarnished because of its continued inability to deal with international terrorism. Israel is especially caustic toward the UN—"this world body with pontificating diplomats." Ambassador Herzog, at the onset of the Security Council debate, said that the issue "is not what Israel did at Entebbe Airport: the issue before this body is its own future in the eyes of history." The UN could retrieve, "in small measure, the prestige and good-will which it has dissipated by becoming hostage to despots and extremists."

Yet, the inability of the UN so far to find a formula to act against international terrorism is not the fault of the UN. It is a reflection of the divergences of international opinion among 144 states. Israel has, in the words of Ambassador Scranton, been "justified" on this issue. But it is ignoble of Israel to tear down the UN, which is but a mirror or a tool. Blame the Arab states, blame those countries that, in the words of Israel, "fail to take a clear and unequivocal stand on this issue for reasons of expediency or cowardice." They may be "despised in history," but not the UN. Indeed, the UN has served and continues to serve a unique purpose by being a forum where these issues can be ventilated even if, to date, they cannot be solved. Perhaps this is the price for the universal nature of the world organization. But would Israel, or the United States, or other current detractors of the UN, have it any other way?

WHAT WASHINGTON WANTS DONE [2]

The item before us is profoundly important. No one can deny that the scourge of terrorism continues to plague the international community and to devastate the innocent.

It is accordingly incumbent upon all governments to join in taking the measures that the international commu-

[2] From "U.S. Calls for Responsible Measures Against International Terrorism," statement by Monroe Leigh, legal adviser, United States Department of State, before Committee VI (Legal) of the UN General Assembly, December 6, 1976. *Department of State Bulletin.* 76:75-7. Ja. 24, '77.

nity can take to deal with this pervasive problem. It is incumbent upon all governments to consider, and act upon,
what can be done to deal with terrorism, for a number of
reasons.

Governments have a paramount obligation to protect
the lives of their citizens. If there is one thing that is clear,
it is that the inherently indiscriminate nature of terrorism
makes it a threat to people everywhere. Not only is the terrorist act itself aimed at taking human lives—often for the
mere publicity value of the act—but the reactions that such
acts inevitably and understandably engender also sometimes result in loss of life. Terrorism is the starting point
of a process which is likely to lead not merely to bloodshed
on a small scale but to a threat to the peace, or worse.

Governments are obligated, moreover, to consider the
effect on their standing and that of the international community of tolerating acts of terrorism. Can any government
worthy of governing be expected to acquiesce in the continuing victimization of its citizens? Can an organized
international community which tolerates acts of terrorism
maintain that measure of self-respect necessary for its simple
survival as an organized international community—still less
its closer and more effective integration? Can the United
Nations be taken seriously as a force for human rights, racial justice, and economic equity if, as an institution, it is
indifferent to internationally promoted murder?

For its part, my government remains concerned. We
believe that the international community should and must
undertake measures to deal with terrorism. We believe
those measures should be grounded on the same humanitarian concerns that underlie laws of war. If we can limit
the conduct permissible to a state which is fighting for its
survival in accordance with its inherent right of self-defense,
we surely can limit actions by groups or individuals which,
whether undertaken for base or noble goals, are not considered legal by states under international law. We certainly
can do so in cases where such acts are of an international

character or where they violate fundamental human rights (as they characteristically do).

United States Draft Convention

The United States submitted a draft convention to the General Assembly in 1972 for the prevention and punishment of certain acts of international terrorism. Our draft was not aimed at all acts of terrorism but only at the spread of terrorism to persons and places removed from the scene of the conflict. We said at that time, and we say now, that we do not maintain that our approach is the only possible approach or the best of all approaches. It is the best approach which we have devised in light of the circumstances. We invite others to support our suggested approach or to propose something better.

We are aware of the objections some have raised to our proposal for a treaty that would attempt to deter the export of terrorism. Briefly put, these objections can be summarized under three headings: (1) that national liberation movements must have a free hand; (2) that governmental action causes death, so why single out acts of other entities; and (3) that there can be no action taken against terrorism until the underlying causes of terrorism are eliminated.

While we have a measure of sympathy and a larger measure of understanding for some of the motives behind some of these arguments, we find them wholly unconvincing—from the standpoint of the progressive development of international law and from the standpoint of the preservation of the peace.

We do not believe that any government disagrees with those humanitarian aspects of the laws of war which limit or endeavor to limit state conduct. If, then, there are horrors and outrages that even states fighting for their lives cannot indulge in, there must be limits to what conduct groups or individuals may indulge in. Indeed, no one has yet argued that groups or individuals may use poison gas or dumdum bullets. The sooner we recognize that we all agree that there are limits on permissible conduct of groups or individuals to use force to promote their objectives, the sooner we can sit down and talk about what those limits are or ought to be. We may wish to set the international limits at one level and another government may wish to set them at another, but that is a matter susceptible to solution by rational discourse. Our plea is that we stop throwing up smokescreens of false argument and sit down to work out humanitarian limits.

Issue of "State Terrorism"

The argument that one cannot take action against groups or individuals without taking action against states—against so-called "state terrorism"—is transparently fallacious. Indeed, we doubt many assert that nihilistic view with genuine conviction. The world is too full of problems, and if we refuse to deal with one of them until we can deal with all of them, we shall never deal with any. For example, our inability to eradicate violations of human rights in all cases —even in all grave cases—cannot be a basis for refusing to try to alleviate human rights violations in southern Africa.

Moreover, we must recognize that there is already in existence an established body of rules governing state conduct. There is the United Nations Charter, with its unarguable prohibition against the threat or use of force. There are the laws of war that govern those situations when fighting nevertheless breaks out. The laws of war have had great humanitarian effect, though at the same time gravely inadequate effect; and of course those imperfect rules are now being revised. But new rules are not needed to inform states when the use of force is permissible and when it is not. And even if new rules were necessary, and achievable, a need to deal with *that* problem would not provide a valid excuse for ignoring others, such as those of international economic order—new, old, or whatever. Nor would it provide a valid excuse for refusing to take measures to deal with terrorism.

The third argument often used to bar examination of possible measures is that we cannot engage in a discussion of practical measures until we eliminate the root causes of terrorism. The very existence of all of our governments indicates how spurious this line of argument is. Crime occurs in all of our countries, bar none. More in some than others, but the society does not exist whose laws are never violated. In many cases, that crime has its roots in social causes. Yet all our governments apprehend, prosecute, and punish criminals. None of our heads of state, parliamentary bodies, or judges urge the elimination of criminal law until the causes of criminal conduct have been eliminated. Repressive governments merely punish those they consider criminal. Responsible governments do not merely punish criminals. They seek to improve the nature of their societies and to insure the widest measure of justice so that punishment is proportionate and the causes of crime are ameliorated.

Were the United Nations to embark on concluding a convention along the lines we suggest, would it be behaving like a repressive government or a responsible one? The answer to that question lies in the immense work that is currently going on throughout the UN system to improve the social situation for all the world's people. Poverty and injustice are being fought directly in more than half of the main committees of the Assembly as well as the Economic and Social Council and the Security Council and the specialized agencies. Like that of most national governments, the record of the United Nations is one of only partial success. If, then, the United Nations could not be said to resemble a repressive government, could it be said to resemble a responsible one? My government does not believe we can give an unqualified affirmative response to that question so long as there is an unwillingness in this body to take responsible measures to deal with the scourge of terrorism.

We respectfully urge all members who care whether the United Nations can be regarded as an organization com-

prised of responsible members to join our efforts to find
measures to control international terrorism. We urge all
members to join in a common effort to protect all mankind
from barbaric acts of violence which have already cost so
many lives to so little purpose.

WILL BARGAINING WORK? [3]

Rockets rip through the United States Embassy in Beirut. . . . An American military adviser is gunned down on
a street in Tehran. . . . In Khartoum, two American diplomats held hostage by Palestinian terrorists are riddled with
machine gun bullets after demands for political concessions
are not met. . . . Caskets containing the bodies of an
American ambassador and his economic counselor are received in Washington by President Ford to a nineteen-gun
salute. . . .

Although the biggest headlines in the rising incidence of
international terrorism have gone to Arab actions against
Israeli nationals, such as the slaying of Israeli athletes at the
1972 Olympics in Munich and the abduction and dramatic
rescue of the passengers of an Air France jet . . . [in Uganda],
American government missions abroad have also been a
primary target. In the 77 episodes from 1968 to 1975 in
which hostages were held for ransom, the victims included
about thirty American officials, six of whom were killed.
And for nearly six years now, Washington has adhered to a
policy of "no concessions" to the terrorists. It will not accede
to demands put forward as a condition for the hostages'
release, it will not negotiate such terms, and it will not put
pressure on other governments to yield. In the interests of
deterring future terrorism, America hangs tough.

But now this rigid policy has come under fire. Critics
within the State Department and elsewhere are calling for

   [3] From "Bargain With Terrorists?" by Judith Miller, Washington correspondent of *The Progressive*. New York *Times Magazine*. p 7+. Jl. 18, '76. © 1976
by The New York Times Company. Reprinted by permission.

a more flexible approach—one that would permit negotiations with terrorists and, under certain circumstances, acquiescence to demands for money and political concessions
to save American lives. This debate over the deterrent value
of the hard-line policy has until recently been shielded from
public view, but now the critics have begun to express their
views more vociferously and publicly.

The Israeli rescue of 103 hijacking hostages and crew
members from Entebbe Airport in Uganda has called attention to the agonizing decisions that confront American
policy makers when American hostages are involved. Fortunately, terrorism is still an insignificant form of violence in
terms of numbers. Between 1968 and mid-1975, only 250
people were killed in terrorist episodes—less than the annual homicide rate of any major American city. But terrorism cannot be measured by statistics. It is violence in its
most pernicious form; its victims are the innocent; it is un-
predictable. And its impact is all the greater because it
makes one's own government seem either helpless or heart-
less—unable to protect its citizens or callous in the remedies
it employs.

The United States has chosen the hard-line approach
well aware of its limitations and liabilities. State Department proponents of this policy know, for instance, that it is
likely to make Washington seem indifferent to the safety of
Foreign Service officials and American citizens abroad. . . .
But unrest within the State Department over the current
stance is growing; there is little ground for hope that acts
of terrorism involving Americans will subside in the near
future, and the whole dilemma is likely to come up for re-
assessment. . . .

Tracing the Development of a "Hard Line"

In the early sixties, terrorist incidents were rare. In 1968,
however, diplomatic kidnappings and attempted assassinations increased markedly in number. Among the victims
that year were four American officials kidnapped and killed

in Latin America and two wounded. Washington dealt with each incident as it occurred; there was no consistent policy. In some cases, the government ignored the terrorists' demands; in others, while refusing to pay ransom, Washington pressed the governments of the countries where the abductions took place to meet the terrorists' conditions. For example, when Ambassador Charles Burke Elbrick was kidnapped in Brazil in 1969, the United States put pressure on Brazil to free fifteen "political prisoners," as demanded by the captors. Brazil reluctantly complied, and the Ambassador was released, unharmed.

In July 1970, Dan Mitrione, an American public-safety adviser stationed in Uruguay, was abducted by the Tupamaros, the "urban guerrillas" then on the rampage in that country. In the developing drama (which has been fictionalized in the Costa-Gavras movie "State of Siege") the Uruguayan government rejected the Tupamaros' offer to release Mitrione in exchange for a group of political prisoners. At this juncture, Washington's policy hardened. As one State Department official said, "We decided not to pressure the Uruguayans to meet the terrorists' demands. We were beginning to realize that such actions would only encourage others to use the same tactic." Efforts to rescue Mitrione were unsuccessful. His dead body was found in an abandoned car.

The number of terrorist incidents rose sharply in 1971, but it was not until the slaughter at the 1972 Olympics that the United States began to take concerted counteraction. President Nixon established a Cabinet Committee to Combat Terrorism. . . . [For organization of committee and cooperating groups see "American Policy Against Terrorism," by Lewis Hoffacker, in Section IV, above.] This group, meeting twice a week, began to lay down plans for coordinated action. What it boiled down to was "no concessions."

On the evening of March 1, 1973, that policy was put to its first major test.

In Khartoum, capital of the Sudan, eight Palestinians of the Black September terrorist faction stormed and seized the Saudi Arabian Embassy during a farewell party for the deputy chief of the American mission, George Curtis Moore. They soon released all their prisoners except two Arab diplomats, the Belgian chargé d'affaires, American Ambassador Cleo A. Noel Jr., and Moore. In exchange for the lives of these five, the Palestinians demanded the release of hundreds of "political prisoners" held in the Mideast and the West—including Sirhan Sirhan, the slayer of Robert Kennedy.

The Working Group in Washington assembled an emergency task force, which set up camp in the State Department's Operations Center, a communications room down the hall from the office of the Secretary of State. Telex messages from the embassy in Khartoum were speeded to various members of the government by phone, pneumatic tube and a facsimile transmitter equipped with a scrambler to insure secrecy. President Nixon sent a Deputy Under Secretary of State, William Macomber Jr., to Khartoum to advise the Sudanese in their negotiations with Black September.

It seemed to many on the task force that there was a chance of saving the hostages' lives. A cable from the embassy in Khartoum said Black September had dropped all its demands except for what seemed to be its bedrock condition—release of seventeen Palestinian guerrillas imprisoned by the Jordanian government after the suppression of the Palestinian commando forces on Jordanian soil. Macomber and his entourage landed in Cairo. The publicity surrounding their mission appeared to have pleased the Palestinians. There were indications that they were prepared to fly to Cairo with their hostages, to continue the negotiations there.

Quite suddenly, things seemed to fall apart. Black September refused to move the talks to the Egyptian capital. Macomber, setting off for Khartoum, was diverted by a sandstorm. The guerrillas issued a "final deadline" for the release of their comrades in Jordan. The Jordanian government refused to comply. At a White House press conference, reporters asked President Nixon about the Sirhan Sirhan demand. He replied that the United States would not give in to blackmail.

We cannot do so and we will not do so [he said]. Now, as to what can be done to get these people released, Mr. Macomber is on his way there for discussions; the Sudanese government is working on the problem . . . but we will not pay blackmail.

The cables to the task force became increasingly ominous. The Palestinians, who, from all indications, were growing anxious and irritated, heard of Nixon's widely reported statement. Soon afterward, they permitted Ambassador Noel to speak by telephone to his embassy. Noel was told Macomber was on his way to Khartoum from Asmara and would arrive later that evening. "That will be too late," the Ambassador said. The next morning, the Palestinians gave themselves up. The bodies of the two Americans and the Belgian were found in the basement.

The new American policy was given more official expression by the President a few days later at a State Department ceremony honoring Noel and Moore.

All of us would have liked to have saved the lives of these two brave men [Nixon said]. But they knew and we knew that in the event we had paid international blackmail, it would have saved their lives, but it would have endangered the lives of hundreds of others all over the world, because once the terrorist has a demand that is made, that is satisfied, he then is encouraged to try it again; that—that is why the position of your Government has to be one, in the interest of preserving life, of not submitting to international blackmail or extortion any place in the world. That is our policy, and that is the policy we are going to continue to have.

Reconsidering the "Hard Line"

The death of the two popular diplomats stunned the Foreign Service. For many in the State Department, the shock was followed by anger. Some felt the handling of the incident had been bungled. Several Foreign Service officers demanded a full-scale study of the Khartoum episode instead of the routine post-mortem conducted by the Working Group. Seven months later, the Rand Corporation, the California-based "think tank," was hired to review the whole question of negotiating for the release of kidnapped diplomats and to make recommendations. Khartoum was one of some thirty cases to be examined. The project was headed by Brian Jenkins, a senior Rand analyst who had long been warning the State Department of the growing threat of terrorism.

Last May [1976], a draft of the report was issued in the form of working notes and was circulated for limited distribution within the State Department. Those familiar with the work describe it as an analysis and indictment of the hard-line policy.

One of the fundamental errors made in the Khartoum incident, according to the draft report, was Nixon's "no blackmail" statement at his White House press conference at the time Macomber was on his way to Khartoum. "The guidance given to him [Nixon], if asked about the affair, was to remain noncommittal," Jenkins wrote. "[The] President's statement . . . suggested that there was not much to negotiate, even when Macomber arrived. . . . [Macomber's] long flight was working as a stall, which the President's statement may have effectively torpedoed." Moreover, Jenkins added, Macomber was sent half-way around the globe from Washington, with the result that no American in a position of authority arrived in Khartoum in time; sending someone closer might have made more sense. And when Macomber *was* dispatched, no one in Washington had a clear idea of what he was supposed to do or why he was being sent.

Among Jenkins's recommendations were that high-level government officials remain silent during such episodes, that all official statements be checked with the task force set up to handle the crisis, and that all information to the press be screened. Even a biographical sketch listing a kidnapped diplomat's previous assignments can have a detrimental impact on his chance of survival, Jenkins argued, since he may have been accredited to a government regarded by the terrorists as their enemy. The Working Group has accepted these recommendations and revised its guidelines accordingly. It has also agreed with his finding that greater expertise and professionalism are required, and it is expanding its membership to include psychiatrists, police specialists and others experienced in "coercive bargaining" with terrorists. The most controversial section of the study, however, deals with the efficacy of the "no-concessions" policy.

The current hard-line position, Jenkins points out, is based on the assumptions that, first, refusing to negotiate, pay ransom or make political concessions deters terrorists from kidnapping American officials; and, second, that any deviation from such a policy would lead to a proliferation of such incidents. Both in his still-classified study and in his public writings, Jenkins contends that the evidence to support these assumptions is "squishy" at best. Terrorism, he reasons, has many objectives; the wringing of concessions is only one of them, and often not the most important; the terrorists may, for example, be hoping to gain publicity for their cause and project themselves as a force that merits recognition. One objective the terrorists do *not* have, he argues, is mass murder. "Terrorists want a lot of people watching and a lot of people listening, not a lot of people dead," he told the House International Relations Committee during hearings . . . [in 1976]. Their target, therefore, is not so much the hostage as the larger audience. In this sense, terrorism is theater. A hard-line policy, while it can add to the theatrical effect, can do little to deter.

It's the Capture Record That Counts

Jenkins has considerable support for his views among other experts on the subject. Professor Richard Falk, of Princeton University, told the same committee, "We don't have real evidence that deterrence works." While agreeing with Jenkins that massacring large numbers of hostages does not fall within the political terrorist's plans, Falk held that in some cases the deaths of some hostages "actually serves the interest of the terrorist group better than would the receipt of ransom demanded (release of prisoners, money, etc.)." Hence, he said, the hard-line policy can often play into the terrorists' hands.

What really deters, according to Jenkins, is not a hard line during the crisis but determined action afterward to capture and convict the terrorists. In this country, he says, there have been only 647 kidnappings for ransom in the past 30 years—and the reason is not far to seek. "If one looks at the record of ransom payment, the ransom has almost always been paid by the family. . . . [But] of the 647 cases, all but three have been solved. The FBI has a better than 90 percent capture record. The conviction rate is extremely high, and the sentences are harsh." Hence the relative unpopularity of kidnapping for ransom within the United States.

This argument is supported by the American Foreign Service Association, the Foreign Service officers' "trade union." The association has established a Committee on Extraordinary Dangers to negotiate with the State Department management on problems of terrorism, and there have been frequent meetings with Kissinger and his top aides. The committee has several objectives.

One is better protection for the 31,000 American officials stationed overseas—and, in that regard, much has been done already. Congress has appropriated $20 million for closed-television monitoring systems, electronic alarms, armored cars, extra Marine guards at American Embassies and other security measures; and American officials—and businessmen living abroad—are briefed on the rudimentary precautions they should take for their own safety. Another demand is for broader medical coverage for former hostages and their families. But the committee's main complaint is against what its members see as the State Department's unwillingness to impose strong sanctions against governments that harbor terrorists or allow them to go free.

The Department's records on that score substantiate the complaint. . . . In the Khartoum case, the Black September guerrillas were convicted of murder and sentenced by the Sudanese to life imprisonment. Soon after, however, all were flown to Egypt, where they are now living under "house arrest." For a brief period, the United States Ambassador to the Sudan was withdrawn and aid was suspended. When the flap died down, normal relations were restored.

"What good is a 'hang tough' posture during a kidnapping," said a Foreign Service committee representative, "if the Department is unwilling to be firm on pressure for punishment? They're perfectly willing to sacrifice us in the name of deterrence, but unwilling to rock the diplomatic boat afterward."

As to the hang-tough policy itself, the Foreign Service has not taken a formal position. Some of its members support it. Others are critical of it, and added their voices to the calls for a more flexible policy that were heard during a two-day conference on international terrorism sponsored by the State Department . . . [in April 1976].

Despite the growing criticism within and outside the government, the State Department clung to the hard-line approach in word and deed.

In May 1973, just a few months after the Khartoum incident, Terrance Leonhardy, United States Consul General in Guadalajara, was kidnapped by left-wing militants who demanded that the Mexican authorities release thirty prisoners and read the kidnappers' communiqué over the air. According to a State Department official familiar with the episode, the United States counseled against acquiescence. But the Mexican government complied with the demands and Leonhardy was released, unharmed.

In March 1974, the United States refused to comply with demands for money made by the kidnappers of Vice Consul John Patterson, stationed in Hermosillo, Mexico. Despite

the efforts of his family to meet the demands, Patterson's
body was found near Hermosillo in July.

During the crisis, Lewis Hoffacker, then head of the
Cabinet Committee to Combat Terrorism, reaffirmed the
"no concessions" policy in congressional hearings. . . . [See
"American Policy Against Terrorism" in Section IV, above.]

In the summer of 1975, three American students were
kidnapped in Tanzania. The ransom was raised by their
families, and the students were released. But the American
Ambassador, W. Beverly Carter Jr., was sternly repri-
manded by Kissinger for his involvement in the negotiations.

It is our policy, in order to save lives and in order to avoid
undue pressure on ambassadors all over the world [Kissinger told
reporters] that American ambassadors and officials not participate
in negotiations on the release of victims of terrorists, and that terrorists know that the United States will not participate in the
payment of ransom and in the negotiations for it. In any individual case, this requires heartbreaking decisions . . . but there
are important issues of principle involved here.

Flexibility Does Not Pay

State Department officials who support that policy insist
that it does deter terrorism. They point out that other governments that have had a more flexible policy—West Germany, the Netherlands and Britain have recently tough-
ened their positions on negotiations and ransom payment.
They argue that kidnappings of diplomats would have increased at an even steeper rate had the United States not
held firm to its position. In the absence of international
agreement on a code of sanctions and punishment—one
man's "terrorist" is, in many instances, another man's "freedom fighter"—it should be, they contend, the obligation of
each government to demonstrate to the terrorists that their
tactics will be unproductive.

The hard-line approach, these officials claim, can sometimes even enhance the victim's own bargaining power. By
way of example they point to the 1974 kidnapping of Bar-

bara Hutchison, of the United States Information Agency, by terrorists in the Dominican Republic who sought the release of imprisoned comrades. She persuaded her captors to free her by convincing them that the United States would never pressure the Dominican government to accede to their demands and that killing her would be pointless.

Actually, the Jenkins recommendations would retain some of the benefits, real or imagined, of the present posture. A flat "no-concessions" policy, he says, limits the range of possible responses and stifles innovative action aimed at saving a hostage's life. Those managing these crisis situations, he contends, should not be forced to rule out any option in advance. Nothing should be prohibited—either negotiating formally, or bargaining informally or secretly, or even paying ransom, if it can be arranged through third parties without publicity. In other words, the United States could continue to espouse a hard line publicly, while becoming more flexible privately.

Jenkins dismisses the objection that such a two-tier policy would readily become apparent in the era of Watergate journalism. Because each incident is unique and complex, there is already a degree of ambivalence and confusion surrounding such episodes. When Colonel . . . [Ernest R.] Morgan was held hostage in Beirut last year, the United States publicly refused to consider ransom. But ransom was paid—ostensibly by a group of unidentified Lebanese businessmen—and the colonel was released. [Colonel Morgan, a black army officer assigned to the United States Advisory Mission to Turkey, was released to safeguard black American relations with the Arab cause, according to a communiqué released by the kidnappers.—Ed.] While Washington officials insist that the United States did not deviate from its "no concessions" line, they concede that speculation about the source of the funds persists. The American government, Jenkins suggests, ought to be able to capitalize on ambivalence of this kind. "To assume that private flexibility would immediately become apparent is to assume gross stupidity and incompetence in the management of such crises."

There is another consideration that is often cited by Jenkins's supporters within the State Department—the difficulty for any government to implement a "no-concessions" policy consistently and evenhandedly. The United States would not negotiate for the lives of Noel and Moore in Khartoum, but would it refuse to negotiate or consider ransom if the hostage were Henry Kissinger or Susan Ford?

Even Israel, regarded as an exemplar of the toughest policy possible, has negotiated with terrorists in several particularly difficult episodes. After an El Al jet was hijacked to Algiers in 1968, Israel agreed to release Arab prisoners as a gesture of "goodwill" to save the plane's crew and passengers. A year later, Israel exchanged two captured Syrian Air Force pilots for two Israeli hostages of a hijacking. The Israelis were also willing to negotiate with the Palestinians for captured Israeli schoolchildren in the town of Ma'alot in 1974. In that instance, deciding the negotiations would not prove fruitful, the Israelis stormed the school and one of the terrorists sprayed the children with bullets, resulting in the death of twenty-four.

The raid on Entebbe Airport has renewed debate within the Administration. Some see the Israeli action as vindicating the hard-line approach. According to this view, the Israeli "negotiations" were merely a shield behind which the government planned its bold and risky mission. Others came to the opposite conclusion. They believe the Israeli officials who insist that the negotiations were serious, and they thus see the talks as a departure from Israel's usual hard-line policy. Whatever the case—and officials here have no hard evidence to contradict the Israeli assertions of good faith—policy makers believe the Israeli response to the hijacking is not relevant to American planning and decision-making. "The option the Israelis chose," said one high-level official, "would never be possible for us." The feeling is that Israel, already a pariah to many in the United

Nations, stood to lose little through such an assault, whereas the United States, as a world power, could not engage in such unorthodox action without suffering a tremendous loss of prestige.

Inhibitions of a "Superpower"

The United States role as superpower, Administration officials argue, also limits the retributive action that Washington can seek against nations harboring terrorists or allowing them to go free. While the United States may like to "punish" such nations, the officials say, broader foreign-policy interests often make the withholding of economic and military aid, or the withdrawal of an ambassador, counterproductive. In addition, given the year-long congressional investigation of the CIA and other intelligence agencies, formation of special squads to hunt down and capture or kill international terrorists has been ruled out as an option. Finally, the United States has publicly supported solutions to international terrorism through the United Nations, and extreme unilateral responses such as the Entebbe mission would not be consistent with the stated American goal of achieving an international consensus.

Therein lies the full painfulness of the dilemma. "Be more flexible, do everything possible to save our people's lives during the crisis—and come down hard afterward on the terrorists and those who support or tolerate their actions," say the critics of the present policy. "But we're already as flexible as we can be," reply the policy makers. "We communicate with the kidnappers through third parties in every way short of negotiation or bargaining. We take advantage of every option we have. The inescapable fact is that some options during and after the crisis are simply not open to us." It is also inescapable that the terrorists are becoming increasingly sophisticated, daring and innovative, and the pressure on the United States government to match them in these attributes can only increase.

THE DANGERS OF OVER-PROTECTION [4]

A society free from the threat of terrorism is quite attainable. Fascist systems manage to reduce terrorism by a series of devices: mass organizations in which membership is compulsory; block-by-block spying networks; mandatory police-identification certificates, and clear delineations of "friends" and "enemies" of the regime.

With the increased sophistication of computerization techniques, such mechanisms for social and personal control loom ever larger. The question is not one of technique but of social policy: Does a citizenry wish to pay such a price for tranquillity?

The acceptance of some terrorism, like some protest violence, is a sign of a society's acceptance of the costs of liberty. The potential for terror is also a reminder that the state's force has its counterforce; and the hardware of the state is almost always greater, more pervasive, and more devastating than the disruptive possibilities that are available to terrorists.

If we evaluate terrorism in terms of the number of people that have been killed by design or by accident, there is clearly no comparison with the genocidal behavior of Stalin in Russia and Hitler in Germany.

The autocratic state has nearly unlimited power to terrorize entire communities, ethnic or racial groups, and, of course, religious networks. If terrorism is judged simply in terms of lives dispatched, the Nazi holocaust—the genocidal benchmark of our century—outstrips the desultory performances engaged in by contemporary terrorists.

If we consider terrorism in terms of its disruption of local political systems or social organizations, again there is scarcely any comparison between what terrorists achieve and the disruption caused by a major automobile accident

[4] From "Dangers to Liberty in Fighting Terrorism," by Irving Louis Horowitz, professor of sociology and political science at Rutgers University. New York Times. p 25. Ap. 30, '77. © 1977 by The New York Times Company. Reprinted by permission.

on an urban superhighway or the large-scale temporary breakdown occasioned by a power failure in a big city. It is the symbolic effect of terrorism that represents its real impact.

When persons are assassinated or kidnapped because of their national origins or religious affiliations, this threatens the entire structure of intergroup toleration and support. Because terrorism involves death and destruction by design, it is clearly different from the random character of highway accidents or technological breakdowns.

Risks as a Measure of Democracy

The measurement of terrorism's success therefore is not only its ability to topple the social order but also its ability to loosen that order in symbolic terms, by weakening the legitimating capacities of elected officials and casting doubt on our concept of the rights of a society and the obligations of a state. [See "Terrorism: Origins and Strategy," by David Fromkin in Section I, above, for a more detailed discussion of the strategy of terrorists and governments' need to comprehend it in order to react effectively. —Ed.]

For example, the act of boarding an airplane involves an acceptance of commonplace procedures that a few short years ago would have been deemed a direct violation of civil liberties. Most people accept the frisking and new baggage procedures as the necessary cost of a safe flight. Nonetheless, one has a perfect right, even a duty, to raise questions about these new social costs of travel, certainly to inquire whether the new frisking procedures are permanent or transitory.

Risk is part of the nature of the democratic system— to permit modes of behavior that are uncontrolled and experimental. To insist that new mechanisms have to be created to prevent terror may be more risky than accepting the possibility of certain terrorist acts.

Under the banner of the anti-terrorist industry (airport·

surveillance equipment, home-security systems, counter-terror research) enormous erosion of civil liberties could be made to seem all too rational and enlightened to the general public. The costliest aspect of terrorism may not be the destruction of physical property and loss of life—as terrorists intend—but the weakening of the social and political fabric, that complex series of norms and laws upon which democratic conflict-resolution ultimately rests. ⟩

BIBLIOGRAPHY

An asterisk (*) preceding a reference indicates that the article or a part of it has been reprinted in this book.

Books, Pamphlets, and Documents

Alexander, Yonah, ed. International terrorism: national, regional, and global perspectives. Praeger. '76.

Bassiouni, M. C. ed. International terrorism and political crimes. C. C. Thomas. '75.

Bell, J. B. Terror out of Zion: the Irgun, Lehi, Stern and the Palestine underground. St. Martin's. '76.
Review. New York Times. p. 25. Je. 27, '77 Terence Smith.

Bell, J. B. Transnational terror. (Hoover Institute Studies, 53) American Enterprise Institute for Public Policy Research. 1150 17th St. N.W. Washington, DC 20036. '75.

Burton, A. M. Urban terrorism: theory, practice and response. Free Press. '76.

Camus, Albert. Neither victims nor executioners. (Modern Classics of Peace Series) World Without War Council. 110 S. Dearborn St. (Suite 820). Chicago, IL 60603. '68.

Carlton, David and Schaerf, Carlo, eds. International terrorism and world security. Wiley. '75.

Clutterbuck, R. L. Living with terrorism. Faber & Faber. '75.

Clutterbuck, R. L. Protest and the urban guerrilla. (Abelard-Schuman Book) Crowell. '74.

Dallin, Alexander and Breslauer, G. W. Political terror in Communist systems. Stanford University Press. '70.

Eggers, William. Terrorism; the slaughter of innocents. Major Books. '75.

Green, Gilbert. Terrorism: is it revolutionary? New Outlook Publishers. '70.

Hacker, F. J. Crusaders, criminals, crazies: terror and terrorism in our time. Norton. '77.

Halperin, Ernst. Terrorism in Latin America. Sage Publications. '76.

Havens, M. C. and others. Assassination and terrorism: their modern dimensions. Sterling Swift. '75.

Hussain, Mehmood. The Palestine Liberation Organization: a study in ideology, strategy and tactics. International Publications Service. '75.

Hyams, E. S. Terrorists and terrorism. St. Martin's. '75.

Jenkins, B. M. High technology terrorism and surrogate war: the impact of new technology on low-level violence. Rand Corporation. 1700 Main St. Santa Monica, CA 90406. '75.

Jenkins, B. M. International terrorism: a new kind of warfare. Rand Corporation. 1700 Main St. Santa Monica, CA 90406. '74.
  Statement before the Subcommittee on the Near East and South Asia, Committee on Foreign Affairs, United States House of Representatives.

Jenkins, B. M. International terrorism: a new mode of conflict. Crescent Publications. '75.

Jenkins, B. M. and Johnson, Janera. International terrorism: a chronology, 1969-1974. Rand Corporation. 1700 Main St. Santa Monica, CA 90406. '75.
  Prepared for the United States Department of State and the Defense Advanced Research Projects Agency.

Laqueur, Walter. Guerrilla: a historical and critical study. Little, Brown. '76.

McKnight, Gerald. The terrorist mind: why they hijack, kidnap, bomb and kill. Bobbs-Merrill. '75.

Merleau-Ponty, Maurice. Humanism and terror; an essay on the Communist problem. Beacon Press. '69.

Moss, Robert. The war for the cities. Coward, McCann and Geoghegan. '72.

Parry, Albert. Terrorism; from Robespierre to Arafat. Vanguard Press. '76.

Piasetzki, J. P. Urban guerrilla warfare and terrorism: a selected bibliography. Council of Planning Librarians. P.O. Box 229. Monticello, IL 61856. '76.

Sobel, L. A. ed. Political terrorism. Facts on File, Inc. 119 W. 57th St. New York 10019. '75.

Stevenson, William and Dan, Uri. Ninety minutes at Entebbe. Bantam. '76.

Teixeira, Bernardo. The fabric of terror; 3 days in Angola. Devin-Adair. '65.

Trotsky, Leon. Against individual terrorism. Pathfinder Press, Inc. '74.

United States. Congress. House of Representatives. Committee on Foreign Affairs. Subcommittee on the Near East and South Asia. International terrorism: hearings; June 11-24, 1974. 93d Congress, 2d Session. Supt. of Docs. Washington, DC 20402. '74.

United States. Congress. House of Representatives. Committee
on Internal Security. Terrorism: hearings, pts. 1-4, February
27-August 20, 1974. 93d Congress, 2d Session. Supt. of Docs.
Washington, DC 20402. '74.

United States. Congress. Senate. Committee on the Judiciary.
Subcommittee to Investigate the Administration of the Internal Security Act and Other Internal Security Laws. Terroristic activity: hearings, pt. 4, May 14, 1975: International
terrorism. 94th Congress, 1st Session. Supt. of Docs. Washington, DC 20402. '75.

United States. Congress. Senate. Committee on the Judiciary.
Subcommittee to Investigate the Administration of the Internal Security Act and Other Internal Security Laws. Terroristic activity: hearings, pt. 5, July 25, 1975: Hostage defense
measures. 94th Congress, 1st Session. Supt. of Docs. Washington, DC 20402. '75.

United States. Congress. Senate. Committee on the Judiciary.
Subcommittee to Investigate the Administration of the Internal Security Act and Other Internal Security Laws. Terroristic activity: hearings, pt. 6, July 30, 1975: The Cuban
connection in Puerto Rico; Castro's hand in Puerto Rican
and U.S. terrorism. 94th Congress, 1st Session. Supt. of Docs.
Washington, DC 20402. '75.

United States. Congress. Senate. Committee on the Judiciary.
Subcommittee to Investigate the Administration of the Internal Security Act and Other Internal Security Laws. Terroristic activity: hearings, pt. 7, October 23, 1975: Terrorist
bombings and law enforcement intelligence. 94th Congress,
1st Session. Supt. of Docs. Washington, DC 20402. '75.

United States. Federal Bureau of Investigation. Bomb summary:
a comprehensive report of incidents involving explosive and
incendiary devices in the nation, January-June 1975. (FBI
Uniform Crime Reports) The Bureau. Washington, DC
20535. '75.

United States. Law Enforcement Assistance Administration.
National Institute of Law Enforcement and Criminal Justice. Terrorism: a selected bibliography; G. D. Boston and
others. Supt. of Docs. Washington, DC 20402. '76.

Walter, E. V. Terror and resistance: a study of political violence,
with case studies of some primitive African communities.
Oxford University Press. '69.

Watson, F. M. Political terrorism: the threat and the response.
Robert B. Luce, Inc. '76. (refer orders to McKay)

Wilkinson, Paul. Political terrorism. Halsted Press. '75.

PERIODICALS

America. 133:378-9. N. 29, '75. Letter from Belfast. C. M. Buckley.
  Reply. America. 134:2. Ja. 10, '76. Seamus O'Shean.
*America. 135:94-7. S. 4, '76. Hostages, hijacking and the Security Council. H. A. Jack.
America. 135:410-12. D. 11, '76. Terrorism and the death penalty. T. P. Thornton.
American Legion Magazine. 98:8-11+. My. '75. The threat of nuclear blackmail: what are the chances of stealing or hijacking fissionable materials for extortion or sabotage? H. A. Perry.
American Legion Magazine. 100:18-21+. Mr. '76. Are terrorists stalking America's Bicentennial? T. A. Hoge.
Army Quarterly and Defence Journal. 106:189-93. Ap. '76. Capital punishment and terrorist murder: the continuing debate. K. O. Fox.
Aviation Week & Space Technology. 104:22-4. Ja. 5, '76. Major effort salvages New York service; La Guardia explosion.
Aviation Week & Space Technology. 105:7. Jl. 12, '76. Israel points the way: Ugandan rescue. Robert Hotz.
Aviation Week & Space Technology. 105:241-2. Jl. 19, '76. U.N. deadlocks on hijacking, rescue.
*Aviation Week & Space Technology. 105:9. Ag. 30, '76. Progress against hijacking. Robert Hotz.
*Aviation Week & Space Technology. 105:23. N. 22, '76. Hijacker, terrorist extradition sought by Council of Europe.
Bulletin of the Atomic Scientists. 31:12-16. My. '75. Terrorists keep out! problem of safe-guarding nuclear materials. Mason Willrich.
Bulletin of the Atomic Scientists. 31:28-34. Je. '75. Terrorists and nuclear technology. D. M. Krieger.
Bulletin of the Atomic Scientists. 31:51. D. '75. International convention against nuclear theft. F. R. Frank.
Bulletin of the Atomic Scientists. 32:33-4. Je. '76. Perfect Trojan horse; threat of nuclear terrorism. D. D. Comey.
Bulletin of the Atomic Scientists. 32:34-5. Je. '76. Potentialities of terrorism. B. L. Cohen.
Bulletin of the Atomic Scientists. 32:7. S. '76. Some questions about Entebbe. S. H. Day Jr.
Bulletin of the Atomic Scientists. 32:29-36. O. '76. Nuclear sabotage. Michael Flood.
Bulletin of the Atomic Scientists. 32:8-9. N. '76. Reflections on modern terrorism. Gerald Holton.

Bulletin of the Atomic Scientists. 32:8-9. N. '76. Third thoughts on Entebbe. Howard Medwed.

Business Week. p 34. Je. 16, '75. Lebanon: business recoils from the violence.

Christian Century. 92:486-7. My. 14, '75. Israeli, Irish and Arab terrorism. Philip Perlmutter.

Christian Century. 93:60-2. Ja. 28, '76. British and the IRA. T. R. Beeson.

Christian Century. 93:651. Jl. 21, '76. Rescue at Entebbe. J. M. Wall.

*Christian Science Monitor. p 3. D. 19, '75. Coming to grips with world terrorism. David Anable.

Commonweal. 103:485-6. Jl. 30, '76. Working both ends of the street; UN reaction to Israeli Entebbe raid. Frank Getlein.

*Current History. 70:27-9. Ja. '76. Terrorism and the nuclear threat in the Middle East. L. R. Beres.

Department of State Bulletin. 72:406. Mr. 31, '75. U.S. deplores terrorist incident in Tel Aviv; statements, March 6, 1975. G. R. Ford; H. A. Kissinger.

*Department of State Bulletin. 74:394-403. Mr. 29, '76. International terrorism; address. R. A. Fearey.

Department of State Bulletin. 75:181-6. Ag. 2, '76. U.S. gives views in Security council debate on Israeli rescue of hijacking victims at Entebbe airport; statements. W. W. Scranton; W. T. Bennett.

Department of State Bulletin. 75:554. N. 1, '76. President Ford signs ratifications of conventions on terrorism; statement, October 10, 1976. G. R. Ford.

*Department of State Bulletin. 76:75-7. Ja. 24, '77. U.S. calls for responsible measures against international terrorism. Monroe Leigh.

Economist. 253:17-18. D. 7, '74. Or such less penalty: if the British start hanging terrorists, they'll be out of Ulster in a year—which is just what the IRA wants.

Economist. 257:9-10. D. 6, '75. Must night fall?

*Foreign Affairs. 53:683-98. Jl. '75. The strategy of terrorism. David Fromkin.

Harper's Magazine. 252:24+. Mr. '76. Fourth estate: Arafat's press agents. W. J. Drummond and Augustine Zycher.

*Harper's Magazine. 252:99-105. Mr. '76. The futility of terrorism. Walter Laqueur.

Harper's Magazine. 253:69-72+. N. '76. Continuing failure of terrorism. Walter Laqueur.

Intellect. 104:551. My. '76. Dealing with terrorist acts. J. B. Bell.

International Problems. 14:24-9. Fall '75. Some perspectives on international terrorism. Yonah Alexander.

Military Review. 56:3-11. Ap. '76. Nuclear terrorism and the Middle East. A. R. Norton.

Military Review. 56:58-68. Jl. '76. The corporals' war: internal security operations in Northern Ireland. N. L. Dodd.

Nation. 221:45-6+. Jl. 19, '75. Basque problem: Guernica lives. Paul Preston.

National Review. 27:978. S. 12, '75. How not to combat terrorism; students kidnapped in Tanzania.

National Review. 28:21-2. Ja. 23, '76. Year of the terrorist.

National Review. 28:834. Ag. 6, '76. Reflections on Entebbe. James Burnham.

New Republic. 173:12-14. Ag. 30, '75. New terrorists; random murder. Michael Walzer.

New Republic. 173:3-5. O. 18, '75. Friends of the IRA.

New Republic. 173:8-10. N. 22, '75. Patty Hearst and the new terror. Roger Morris.

*New Republic. 173:10-12. N. 22, '75. The gun in Europe. J. B. Bell.

*New Republic. 173:12-15. D. 27, '75. Terrorism: a debate. Michael Walzer, J. B. Bell, Roger Morris.

New Republic. 174:17-19. Je. 19, '76. Northern Ireland. J. B. Bell.

New York Times, sec IV, p 3. Ag. 17, '75. The world's terrorists sometimes are united. Robert Fisk.

*New York Times. p E1. Jl. 11, '76. With life at stake, how can terrorists be dealt with? Terence Smith.

*New York Times. p E2. Ja. 23, '77. Bonn wasn't eager to extradite Abu Daoud. C. R. Whitney.

New York Times. p 33. Mr. 19, '77. Hanafi seizure fans new debate on press coverage of terrorists. Carey Winfrey.

*New York Times. p 25. Ap. 30, '77. Dangers to liberty in fighting terrorism. I. L. Horowitz.

New York Times. p 7. Je. 15, '77. Vance takes theme of rights to O.A.S. Alan Riding.

New York Times. p 31. Je. 28, '77. The C.I.A., Cuba and terrorism. John Marks.

New York Times. p 31. Je. 28, '77. The infection of terrorism. Walter Goodman.

New York Times Magazine. p 12-13+. F. 4, '73. Ultimate blackmail; atomic blackmail. R. E. Lapp.

New York Times Magazine. p 14-15+. My. 11, '75. Ulrike & Andreas; Baader-Meinhof gang. M. J. Lasky.

*New York Times Magazine. p 7+. Jl. 18, '76. Bargain with terrorists? Judith Miller.

New York Times Magazine. p 8-9+. Jl. 25, '76. Fear in paradise. Stephen Davis.

Newsweek. 85:20. F. 10, '75. Bombs away; bombings by the Weather underground.

Newsweek. 86:40+. Jl. 14, '75. Terror incorporated. Raymond Carroll and Scott Sullivan.

Newsweek. 86:29. O. 6, '75. Now, the violent woman. K. L. Woodward and Phyllis Malamud.

Newsweek. 86:36-7. D. 22, '75. To catch a terrorist; police tactics. Raymond Carroll and others.

Newsweek. 87:24-6. Ja. 5, '76. Year of terror. Raymond Carroll and others.

Newsweek. 87:31+. Ja. 12, '76. Everything blew; bombing at La Guardia airport, New York City. Sandra Salmans and others.

Newsweek. 87:40. My. 17, '76. Animal squad: anti-Soviet violence by Jewish groups in New York City. D. A. Williams and others.

Newsweek. 87:45. Je. 7, '76. Death squads. Angus Deming and Robert Cox.

Newsweek. 88:51. Jl. 26, '76. Amin loses another one; U.N. refusal to condemn Israeli raid. Raymond Carroll.

Newsweek. 88:32+. Ag. 2, '76. Assassination in Dublin; killing of British ambassador C. T. E. Ewart-Biggs. M. R Benjamin and others

Newsweek. 88:50-1. Ag. 23, '76. Entebbe II; attack by the Popular front for the liberation of Palestine on El Al passengers in Istanbul airport. Mark Stevens and others.

Newsweek. 88:28. S. 6, '76. Egypt's Entebbe; freeing hostages of hijacked Egyptian airliner in Luxor. William Schmidt.

Newsweek. 88:25. S. 20, '76. Skyjacking for Croatia. D. M. Alpern.

Newsweek. 88:54. S. 27, '76. Exit Carlos.

Newsweek. 88:53-4. N. 1, '76. Cuban connection; coordination of the united revolutionary organizations. Angus Deming and others.

Newsweek. 88:35. D 27, '76. Man in the box; kidnapping of Richard Oetker outside Munich.

Orbis. 19:1309-25. Winter '76. Negotiating for hostages: a policy dilemma. E. F. Mickolus.

Orbis. 19:1326-43. Winter '76. The U.S. response to terrorism against international civil aviation. R. G. Bell.

Police Chief. 42:55-8. S. '75. The hostage situation: exploring the motivation and the cause. C. V. Hassel.

Reader's Digest. 107:84-93. Jl. '75. Northern Ireland: the endless war. David Reed.

*Reader's Digest. 107:73-7. N. '75. Terrorism on the rampage. R. S. Strother and E. H. Methvin.

Reader's Digest. 109:64-9. Ag. '76. Terror on Train 734; hostages taken by South Moluccan guerrillas. Edward Hughes.

Reader's Digest. 109:122-8. O. '76. Rescue at Entebbe; how the Israelis did it.

Saturday Review. 3:4. F. 7, '76. Total power and total madness. Norman Cousins.

Senior Scholastic. 109:22-5. O. 7, '76. International terrorism.

Survey. 20:1-40. Autumn '74. Kidnapping to win friends and influence people. Roberta Wohlstetter.

*TV Guide. 24:2-6; 10-13. Jl. 31, Ag. 7, '76. Terrorism and television. Neil Hickey.

Time. 105:42+. My. 5, '75. Standing up to the gang; takeover of West German embassy in Stockholm by supporters of the Baader-Meinhof gang.

Time. 106:50+. O. 20, '75. Hostage dilemma.

Time. 106:36+. N. 3, '75. Adding up to an epidemic.

Time. 107:40+. Ja. 5, '76. Kidnapping in Vienna, murder in Athens.

Time. 107:33. My. 24, '76. Disciple of despair; suicide of Ulrike Meinhof triggers terrorist attacks.

Time. 107:33. My. 24, '76. Murder in Paris; assassination of Bolivian ambassador, Joachim Zenteno Anaya.

Time. 107:37-8. Je. 14, '76. Murders continue; killing of prominent exiles in Argentina.

Time. 107:39. Je. 21, '76. Death before lunch; murder of Genoa Chief Prosecutor Francesco Coco.

Time. 108:28+. Jl. 12, '76. Battling against subversion.

Time. 108:26+. Ag. 2, '76. Trial by fire in Dublin; killing of C. Ewart-Biggs.

UN Chronicle. 13:15-21+. Ag. '76. Council fails to adopt draft resolution after considering Uganda hijacking issue.

UN Chronicle. 13:40-2. O. '76. Secretary-General calls for urgent attention to question of international terrorism; excerpts from press conference, September 16, 1976. Kurt Waldheim.

U.S. News & World Report. 78:25-6. Mr. 17, '75. World terrorism flares anew—nothing seems to stop it.

U.S. News & World Report. 79:76. S. 29, '75. Around the globe —outbreaks of terror.

*U.S. News & World Report. 79:77-9. S. 29, '75. Terrorism: "growing and increasingly dangerous," interview with R. A. Fearey.

*U.S. News & World Report. 79:22. O. 6, '75. Drive to root out U.S. terror gangs.

U.S. News & World Report. 79:17-18. D. 29, '75. For Northern Ireland, a bloody Christmas. Robin Knight.

U.S. News & World Report. 80:27-8. Ja. 5, '76. Clearer than ever: no sure way to handle global terrorists; who they are, what they've done.

*U.S. News & World Report. 80:58. Ja. 12, '76. Can airports be safe from terror bombings?

U.S. News & World Report. 81:29-32. D. 6, '76. Cuban extremists in U.S. a growing terror threat.

*Vital Speeches of the Day. 41:266-8. F. 15, '75. The U.S. government response to terrorism; address. Lewis Hoffacker.

Vogue. 166:80+. Mr. '76. Londoners fight bombs: cheery bravery or steel shutters? J. J. Buck.

Wall Street Journal. p 1+. O. 24, '75. Beirut's street battle causing many firms to seek safer bases. Ray Vicker.

Wall Street Journal. p 1+. My. 25, '76. War of nerves: Ulster town rebuilds in despair after latest series of bombings; vulnerable Newtownbutler, on the border, remains tensely fearful of IRA. Bowen Northrup.

*Wall Street Journal. 189:1+. Ja. 4, '77. For world's alienated, violence often reaps political recognition. J. A. Tannenbaum.

*Wall Street Journal. 189:1+. Ja. 6, '77. Bitterness surrounding Dutch train hijacking lingers a year later. William Mathewson.

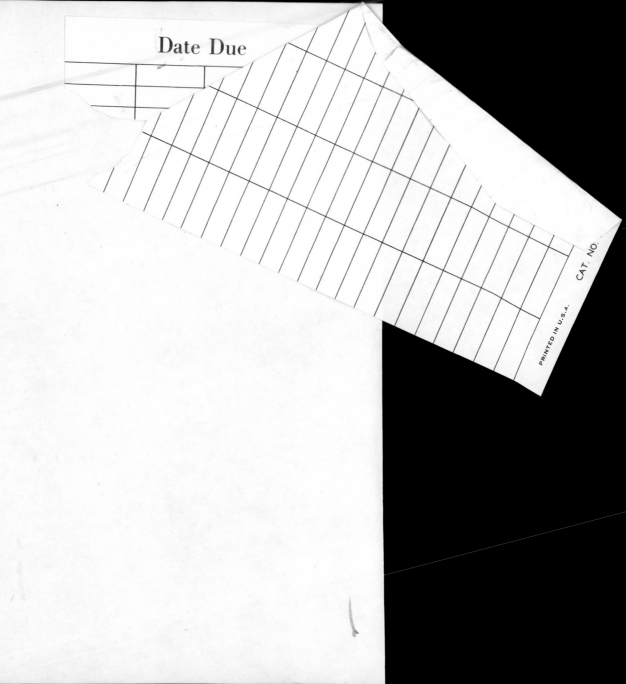

Date Due